The Journey Back to the Father's House

The Journey Back to the Father's House

Joel S. Goldsmith

Edited by
Lorraine Sinkler

Acropolis Books, Publisher
Atlanta, Georgia

Published by Acropolis Books
All rights reserved
Printed in the United States of America

For information contact:
ACROPOLIS BOOKS, INC.
Atlanta, Georgia

www.acropolisbooks.com

Cover and text design: Tonya Beach Creative Services

―――――――――――――――――――

Goldsmith, Joel S., 1892-1964.
 The journey back to the Father's house / Joel S. Goldsmith ; edited by
Lorraine Sinkler.
     p. cm.
 Includes bibliographical references.
 ISBN 1-889051-68-3 (alk. paper)
 1. Spiritual life. I. Sinkler, Lorraine. II. Title.

BP610.G641575 2004
299'.93--dc22

                              2004012383

Except the Lord build the house,
they labour in vain that build it. . .

— Psalm 127

⁀

"Illumination dissolves all material ties and
binds men together with the golden chains of
spiritual understanding; it acknowledges only
the leadership of the Christ; it has no ritual or
rule but the divine, impersonal universal Love;
no other worship than the inner Flame that is
ever lit at the shrine of Spirit. This union is the
free state of spiritual brotherhood. The only
restraint is the discipline of Soul; therefore, we
know liberty without license; we are a united
universe without physical limits, a divine
service to God without ceremony or creed. The
illumined walk without fear – by Grace."

—*The Infinite Way* by Joel S. Goldsmith

Dedication

Twentieth century mystic Joel S. Goldsmith revealed to the Western world the nature and substance of mystical living that demonstrated how mankind can live in the consciousness of God. The clarity and insight of his teachings, called the Infinite Way, were captured in more than thirty-five books and in over twelve hundred hours of tape recordings that, today, perpetuate his message.

Joel faithfully arranged to have prepared from his class tapes, monthly letters which were made available as one of the most important tools to assist students in their study and application of the Infinite Way teachings. He felt each of these letters came from an ever-new insight that would produce a deeper level of understanding and awareness of truth as students worked diligently with this fresh and timely material.

Each yearly compilation of the *Letters* focused on a central theme, and it became apparent that working with an entire year's material built an ascending level of consciousness. The *Letters* were subsequently published as books, each containing all the year's letters. The publications became immensely popular as they proved to be of great assistance in the individual student's development of spiritual awareness.

Starting in 1954, the monthly letters were made availiable to students wishing to subscribe to them. Each year of the *Letters* was published individually during 1954 through 1959 and made available in book form. From 1960 through 1970 the *Letters* were published and renamed as books with the titles:

1960 Letters	*Our Spiritual Resources*
1961 Letters	*The Contemplative Life*
1962 Letters	*Man Was Not Born to Cry*
1963 Letters	*Living Now*
1964 Letters	*Realization of Oneness*
1965 Letters	*Beyond Words and Thoughts*
1966 Letters	*The Mystical I*
1967 Letters	*Living Between Two Worlds*
1968 Letters	*The Altitude of Prayer*
1969 Letters	*Consciousness Is What I Am*
1970 Letters	*Awakening Mystical Consciousness*

Joel worked closely with his editor, Lorraine Sinkler, to ensure each letter carried the continuity, integrity, and pure consciousness of the message. After Joel's transition in 1964, Emma A. Goldsmith (Joel's wife) requested that Lorraine continue working with the monthly letters, drawing as in the past from the inexhaustible tape recordings of his class work with students. The invaluable work by Lorraine and Emma has ensured that this message will be preserved and available in written form for future generations. Acropolis Books is honored and privileged to offer in book form the next eleven years of Joel's teaching.

The 1971 through 1981 *Letters* also carry a central theme for each year, and have been renamed with the following titles:

1971 Letters	*Living by the Word*
1972 Letters	*Living the Illumined Life*
1973 Letters	*Seek Ye First*
1974 Letters	*Spiritual Discernment: the Healing Consciousness*
1975 Letters	*A Message for the Ages*
1976 Letters	*I Stand on Holy Ground*
1977 Letters	*The Art of Spiritual Living*
1978 Letters	*God Formed Us for His Glory*
1979 Letters	*The Journey Back to the Father's House*
1980 Letters	*Showing Forth the Presence of God*
1981 Letters	*The Only Freedom*

Acropolis Books dedicates this series of eleven books to Lorraine Sinkler and Emma A. Goldsmith for their ongoing commitment to ensure that these teachings will never be lost to the world.

Table of Contents

1 Meditation: Its Function and Purpose

19 Letting the Seed Take Root

37 Attaining the Christ-Mind

53 The Temple

71 The Function of the Christ in Us

89 What Have You in the House?

107 Living Out From Conscious Oneness

125 Special Lesson on Healing Work

143 The Spiritual Kingdom Made Tangible

161 God Dominion: Not Man's Domination

181 Unconditioning the Mind

201 Spiritual Preparation for Peace

219 About the Series

221 Scriptural References and Notes

227 Tape Recording References

The Journey Back to the Father's House

Chapter One

Meditation: Its Function and Purpose

I am the vine, ye are the branches.
He that abideth in me, and I in him,
the same bringeth forth much fruit:
for without me ye can do nothing.

If a man abide not in me,
he is cast forth as a branch,
and is withered; and men gather them,
and cast them into the fire, and they are burned.
John 15:5,6

The human race is like the branch of a tree that is cut off and is dying, dying in disease, in sin, or in war. It is always going through a dying process. Rarely have human beings known long periods of peace, long periods of health, or long periods of happiness, and the reason is that they are cut off from the source of life. While we are living a purely human life, we live as if each one of us is a branch, but each one separate from the other, and each one separate from the Creator.

We turn to the spiritual life to be reunited with our source, to live once again in "the secret place of the most High,"[1] to abide in the Word and let the Word abide in us. Immediately, the question arises as to how this is accomplished. In past years many people believed that if they attended a church or if they lived the life of a good Christian or a good Hebrew they were abiding in the Word and would receive the blessing of God.

Human Goodness, No Assurance of Spirituality

Many people have believed that if they prayed a great deal they would be under the government of God. This certainly has not been true when we consider what has often happened to good human beings, even when they go to church or pray regularly. The mere act of being a good human being does not bring one under God's blessing or law. Being a good Christian or a good anything else in the religious world does not ensure that a person will receive the protection of God, the supply of God, the health or the grace of God. All this is a matter of history throughout the centuries.

Christ Jesus himself told the Hebrews that being good, and even being good Jews, was not sufficient:

> For I say unto you, That except your
> righteousness shall exceed the righteousness
> of the scribes and Pharisees, ye shall in no case
> enter into the kingdom of heaven.
>
> Matthew 5:20

The scribes and the Pharisees were perhaps the best Hebrews in the entire synagogue, and yet that was not enough. He even went to far as to say that although John the Baptist was the greatest of all the Hebrew prophets, "he that is least in the kingdom of heaven is greater than he."[2] In other words, his living up to the laws of the church and the rules of the church did not constitute the ingredients that would gain him God's grace.

How Do We Become Children of God?

Paul brought the same thing to light when he said,

> So then they that are in the flesh
> cannot please God. . . .
>
> For as many as are led by the spirit of God,
> they are the sons of God. . . .
>
> The Spirit itself beareth witness with our spirit,
> that we are the children of God. . . .
>
> Romans 8:8, 14, 16

Only if we become children of God are we under the law and grace of God, under the blessing of God. So, as we trace the history of what might be called righteous people, it becomes clear that it is not necessarily those who live up to church rules and church regulations who are the righteous but those who have in some way received in them the spirit of God. If the spirit of God dwell in us, then we become the children of God. When the spirit of God dwells in us, as children of God we become "joint-heirs with Christ."[3] There is always this *if:* if the spirit of God dwells in us, then we become the children of God.

Strangely enough, we have overlooked a great deal of the Master's teaching. He made it clear that we do not become children of God by going to holy mountains or holy temples, that we do not find the kingdom of God in these holy mountains and holy temples because "the kingdom of God cometh not with observation: Neither shall they say, Lo here! or, Lo there! for, behold, the kingdom of God is within you."[4]

This may not sound like a radical teaching, but I assure you it is so radical that if we understood it correctly, and had not heard it before, and began to change our life, we would find that it is not a simple thing to come under the law of God and to receive God's grace. There are many steps to be taken before the spirit of God dwells in us.

First of all, we are not going to get the spirit of God by going some place, nor are we going to get the spirit of God merely by being a good human being. The Master left a blue-print for us to show us how we can come under God's grace. One of the ways he pointed out is that, instead of spending all our time praying for our friends, we must pray for our ene-mies. This we have neglected to do. We have forgotten that we do not become children of God by praying for ourselves, our friends, or our relatives. We become children of God when we begin to pray for our enemies. It is very clearly stat-ed in scripture:

> Pray for them which despitefully use you,
> and persecute you; That ye may be the children
> of your Father which is in heaven.
>
> Matthew 5:44,45

Again we are told that, instead of praying where we can be seen of men, we have to learn to pray secretly, silently, sacredly. We have to enter into a sanctuary, not in a holy mountain or a temple, but in the sanctuary within ourselves for "the kingdom of God is within" us. We have to enter into prayer within our-selves and we must let no man see us praying, nor should we tell any man about our praying:

> And when thou prayest,
> thou shall not
> be as the hypocrites are: for they love to pray
> standing in the synagogues and
> in the corners of the streets,
> that they may be seen of men. Verily I say unto you,
> they have their reward.
> But thou, when thou prayest, enter into thy closet,

and when thou hast shut thy door,
pray to thy Father which is in secret; and thy Father
which seeth in secret shall reward thee openly.

Matthew 6:5,6

So, too, when we do alms, when we give to charity, we must be careful to do our benevolences secretly, not to be seen of men, not to receive the praise of men because of our charity.

The Father Within Knows the Intents of the Heart

As this became clear to me, I caught a vision, which I would like to give you now. There is a Father, there is a divine presence within us, within our own consciousness. Way down deep inside of us is His presence. We can call It by any name we like, whether the presence of God, the presence of the Christ, or the presence of the spirit of God but we must never forget that It is within us. If we are to be in the presence of God however, if we are to benefit by the power of God, we must make contact with this presence within ourselves.

This presence within us cannot be fooled. It has no interest in how holy we appear to be outwardly. It has no interest in what laws we obey outwardly. It has no interest in what we seem to be or pretend to be outwardly. This Father within, this divine presence, knows without question what is taking place in our hearts. It pays no attention to what we say with our lips.

Throughout these past thousands of years, most of the praying that has been done with the lips has gone unanswered and unrewarded. People have been praying for peace, prosperity, health, and safety for countless thousands of years, and they are facing just as much war and just as many accidents, just as much disease, and just as much sin as at any time in all history.

The lesson that was shown me in all this was that there is no use saying anything, thinking anything, or trying to pretend to be something. That which is within us knows, and It searches our heart and our mind. The light of truth is flashed inside of us, and our hidden thoughts, our hidden secrets, and our hidden deeds are known, even if our nearest and dearest never suspect us. This that is within us knows. Our Father that sees in secret rewards us openly. It knows the intents and purposes of our hearts.

The Prayer of Silence

Prayer, therefore, need not have any words or thoughts, because the divine presence knows all about what we say or think, even before we ask, even before we speak. It is folly to waste time thinking thoughts and speaking words when all we need to do is to be silent and let this light that is within us search "the joints and marrow, and [be] a discerner of the thoughts and intents of the heart."[5] We are rewarded in accord with what we really are, not what we pretend to be outwardly.

Students of the Infinite Way are taught the importance of meditating and of beginning with at least three or four times every day. Each meditation period should be three, four, five, six, or seven minutes, or even less to begin with, and then gradually, as meditation becomes easier, more natural, the number of times each day and the length of time spent in each meditation may be increased.

Meditation is not made up of words and thoughts, because we cannot fool God. We may just as well be still and let God search inside us and know what is going on. Our meditation is an inner communion. It has to be the recognition that the Father is within us. Therefore, when we close our eyes, we are shutting out the outside world and we are, even if we do not say it or think it, meaning:

Here I am, Father, coming to You within me for communion that I may know Thee aright. For to know Thee aright is life eternal.[6] So I come to You, Father, to become acquainted with You. I lean not unto my own understanding. How can I acquaint myself with You and be at peace? By recognizing that You are within me. So here I am, Father: I in Thee and Thou in me, and we are one here where I am.

In a public building, in my home, in some church with an open door, in a library, in my automobile, or on a train or bus, wherever I am, Father, Thou art, for Thou art here within me. I am in Thee and Thou art in me, for we are one.

I am here in meditation to know Thee aright. I am not asking for favors; I am seeking to know Thee aright, to commune with Thee, to feel the assurance of Thy presence. I have lived too long without Thee, and I have not made too much of a success of my life. Sometimes my understanding has not been up to my problems; sometimes my virtues have not been up to what is demanded of a person in this world; sometimes my strength has not been sufficient for the problems of the day; sometimes my fears have been too great; sometimes my doubts have gotten in the way of harmonious living; and this only means that I have been living separate and apart from Thee.

Now I seek to know Thee and to feel Thee within me. If only I could feel Thy presence, I would have the courage to face any situation in life. If only I could feel Thy presence, I would be able to fulfill my obligations to my family, to my business, to my nation, to the world. Alone, I cannot achieve this. Thy grace is my sufficiency in all things, but I must have the assurance of Thy grace. I must feel Thy presence; I must know, not merely declare It because it is written in a book; I must feel It. I must experience It.

The Master, Thy beloved son, has taught, "I can of mine own self do nothing.[7] . . . The Father that dwelleth in me, he doeth the works."[8] That is why I am meditating. I am not sufficient unto myself, except when I have Thy presence, Thy grace, Thy wisdom. Thy wisdom is infinite. How then can I rely only on my wisdom? Thy strength is perfect. How can I rely on my strength alone?

I have been living without the assurance of Thy presence. So I am here in meditation to know Thee aright and to acquaint now myself with Thee, to feel an inner oneness with Thee.

This place where I am seems to be so human and so material, but this very place whereon I stand is holy ground, for Thou art here. Thou art within me; Thy presence is with me; Thy presence goes before me, Thy presence is my rock, my foundation, my dwelling place. I live and move and have my being in Thee, and in this meditation I acknowledge that where I am, Thou art. "If I ascend up into heaven, thou art here: If I make my bed in hell, behold, thou art there.[9] . . . Though I walk through the valley of the shadow of death," [10] Thou art there.

Thy presence is the very health of my countenance. Thy presence is my food, my substance, my sustenance. Thy presence is my safety and my security. Thy presence assures me of peace on earth. "My peace I give unto you." [11] And how was this meant? If the kingdom of God is within me, then it is the voice of God that says to me, "My peace I give unto you: not as the world giveth."[11] Thou, Father within me, are assuring me Thou wilt never leave me or forsake me. I never can be outside the kingdom of God, as long as I am abiding in this Word and letting this Word abide in me.

When we abide in the Word, as we have been doing in this meditation, letting these words pour through, we are veritably in God's presence, and God's presence is in us. Then the Ninety-first Psalm comes to life, and none of the evils of the world will come nigh our dwelling place, because we have been dwelling "in the secret place of the most High." [12] We have been living in the presence of God with us, living in the word of God. If we live in the word of God and if we let the word of God live in us, the spirit of God then dwells in us.

After we have reminded ourselves of these things, we can turn within and say, "Speak, Lord; for thy servant heareth."[13] Then, for a minute or two, we become completely silent and listen.

Eventually we learn that God is not in the whirlwind; God is not in the problem; God is not out here in the world: God is in the "still small voice,"[14] the voice that comes to bring to us the assurance, "Son, thou art ever with me, and all that I have is thine,"[15] or "Son, My presence goes before thee to 'make the crooked places straight'."[16] Always there will come some inner assurance of God's presence.

Forgiveness Removes the Barrier

There are times when we begin a meditation of that kind, and then something reminds us that we are violating the law of God or that we are not obeying some law of God. We may be reminded that we are holding anger or resentment against some person, or that we are not forgiving "seventy times seven."[17] Then there is no use praying because unforgiveness is a barrier to our receiving God's grace.

Before we meditate we must first turn within and do the act of forgiving or the act of praying for those who despitefully use us or persecute us, turn within and consciously release all men from any antagonism that we may be feeling. We release everybody who may have harmed us, our family, or our nation.

> "Father, forgive them, for they know not
> what they do."[18] Father, open their eyes that
> they may see; open their ears that they may hear.
> Father, give them light.

Then we can return to our meditation feeling that now we have naught against anyone, and it is not possible for anyone to have aught against us, nor does it matter if they think they have. Once we have forgiven them, we have obeyed the scripture and no longer seek vengeance, "an eye for an eye and a tooth for a tooth,"[19] because of wrongs done to us but have forgiven "seventy times seven." Then there is no barrier between God and us and we are open to receive God's grace.

Becoming Free of Ancient Superstitions

Each time we meditate something entirely new and different may enter our consciousness to remind us of the nearness of God, of the presence, the wholeness and the perfection of God. Sometimes experiences come to us of a very startling nature. They may wake us out of the belief that God punishes sin and rewards goodness. As long as we accept such superstitious beliefs, we cannot enter the kingdom of God. God does not punish and God does not reward.

Jesus taught that God forgives even the woman taken in adultery, not after many years of punishment but now, right now in the instant when she seeks it, forgiveness is there: "Neither do I condemn thee."[20] To the thief on the cross the Master said, "Today shalt thou be with me in paradise."[21] The whole of the Master's teaching is forgiveness, not punishment. Some of us may have been taught that our troubles come to us through God, and that for some reason God has visited this affliction upon us. That is utter nonsense.

The Master reveals that he came to do the will of God, and the will of God is forgiveness "seventy times seven," the healing of disease, the raising from the dead. So it may be a shock when we go into meditation and discover that we are still believing that God has visited death on a person or God has called some loved one home. When we wake up to that, we instantly ask God to forgive us for our ignorance of the truth that the nature of God is love and life eternal in which there is no death. God has "no pleasure in the death of him that dieth. . . wherefore turn yourselves, and live ye."[22]

The whole life of the Master was devoted to raising the sick to health, never once telling them that they were under punishment for some sin, raising them from the dead, proving that God never brought about their death and never approved of their death, since the mission of the Christ is to raise us from the dead. Sometimes when we go into meditation, we find that we have been dwelling on these old ancient beliefs, living in the consciousness prior to two thousand years ago.

To Understand the Nature of God Is to Love God

In our meditation, we have an opportunity to cleanse and purify ourselves of any untrue thoughts that we have been entertaining about God. Before we become more proficient in meditation, our greatest source of joy is the love that develops in our heart for God. People all over the world testify to their love for God. But do they really love God? Nobody loves God who fears God; nobody loves God who believes that God may strike him dead; nobody loves God who believes that God may bring him a disease; nobody loves God who believes that God may punish.

We should love God and trust God more than we trust our own mother. We would not love even our own mother if we thought she had the power or inclination to strike us dead, give us a terrible disease, cause a disastrous accident, or make us lose our money. We could not even love our mother under those conditions and certainly we could not love God.

Love for God comes when we know that God is love and in Him there is no hate, no punishment, no unforgiveness. In Him there are no human qualities, but only the divine qualities of love, forgiveness, joy, raising up from sin, raising up from disease, raising up from death, never pushing us down. Then there comes a love in the heart, and we really can say that we love the Lord our God with all our heart, with all our soul, and with all our mind, because we have no fear of God.

We have no questions about what God will do at any moment or under any circumstances because we know that God is love, and God is in the midst of us. Love is in the midst of us. Love prepares the way for us. Love supports, maintains, and sustains us, and when we make mistakes, as humanly we must do, it is God that forgives, God that raises up, God that says, "Go and sin no more. . . . Neither do I condemn thee." Who but God could voice that to us? Could man forgive us if man did not have God in his heart? And when man forgives us, be assured it is only the God in his heart that causes him to forgive.

We cannot forgive those who have done evil unto us or unto ours, unless we have God in our heart and God can say to us, "Neither do I condemn thee." Then we can say to another, "And neither do I." We can forgive, because all that the Father can do, we can do by His grace, by His love. God's love in us enables us to do what of ourselves we cannot do. The Father within us does the work: the Father within us heals; the Father within us raises up; the Father within us assures us that even if we have fallen down seventy times seven, there will still be another opportunity to go forward. These are the thoughts that may go through our minds in meditation, and thousands more like them. Then we know how to love the Lord our God with all our heart, and that love we feel for God comes right back to us from within us.

One Power

One of the greatest teachings ever given to us by the Master is the teaching of one power, the teaching that there is no power directed against God; there is no power that He has to overcome. God is the all-power and the only power. Most religions have taught us to think of God as some great power that under certain circumstances can overcome evil powers. Even though we see little evidence of it in this world, at least we are taught He can.

The Master never taught that God overcomes evil powers: the Master taught that evil has no power. So great was his conviction that he was able to say to Pilate, the great temporal power of his day, "Thou couldest have no power at all against me, except it were given thee from above."[23] The Master recognized God's allness by realizing that nothing else had power.

There are times when we go into meditation that we are confronted with something that to us is an evil power: some form of illness; some form of lack or limitation; bad business; something concerning our national or international life. It would not be threatening us at all unless we believed that it had power. As a matter of fact we would not even pay any attention to it.

Sitting comfortably in our homes or in some place of worship, we do not pray that God do something to some evil person. We are satisfied that there are no evil persons. Therefore we do not bother to look around for a great power to do something. We recognize that there is only one power, and that is love. When we sit down to meditate, there may be a problem of health, supply, or a national problem. We deal with it in meditation in some fashion as this:

> Father, what is this?
> What is the nature of this problem?
> What is the solution to this problem?

As we meditate again something within us reminds us:

> Fear not; *I* am with you. Fear not,
> they have only the "arm of flesh."[24] Fear not;
> My presence goes with you.
> Fear not; this could have no power over you
> except the power came from *Me*.
> Do not fear anything or anybody.

Sometimes with our problem staring us in the face or waiting to do so when we open our eyes, it may come in another way.

> Fear not; it is *I*. *I* in the midst of you am
> the only power. Be not afraid; it is *I*. Do not fear any

appearances. Do not fear "man,
whose breath is in his nostrils." [25]
Do not fear what man can do to you.
I am in the midst of you. Trust in *Me.*

Through Meditation, the Problem Dissolves

In such a meditation, the word of God comes. Truth comes, and then when we resume our activities in the world, the problem has a way of dissolving, because in that meditation we received the assurance that there are not two powers battling one against another, but that this power that is within us, the kingdom of God within us, is the only power.

Even if we look out and see a Pilate, an enemy, even if we look out and see a sin or a disease, instantly the word of God comes to us and reminds us, "Be not afraid, it is *I. I* am with you. *I* will never leave you or forsake you." The fear dissolves, and when the fear dissolves the whole picture dissolves.

We can read the words of scripture or the words in metaphysical, spiritual, or mystical books, but words in a book have no power. The only power they may have is when they enable us to silence the mind so that in meditation we can go within to our source, and there receive the word of God. Then the armies of the aliens just disappear; they dissolve; they fade away from the face of the earth.

The truth of the kingdom of God within us is a basic principle. Since the kingdom of God is within us, we must learn to go within and acquaint now ourselves with this God who is within and learn about His function in our life, so that never again do we fear punishment or separation because "neither death, nor life. . . shall be able to separate us from the love of God."[26]

Meditation sets us free from the fears and the dangers of this world and brings to light divine harmony, divine grace.

TAPE RECORDED EXCERPTS
Prepared by the Editor

Nothing is more important to ensure the success, fulfillment, and harmony of our experience than to begin each day
with a meditation to establish oneself in the conscious awareness
of God as the one power and one presence, omnipresent, so that
God is no longer a word in the mind but an experience. The
excerpts below will help to point the direction such morning
meditations might take and what might be included in them.

Conscious Awareness

"Every phase of discord that comes into our experience is
a mesmeric influence from which we do not know how to
protect ourselves. In other words, when you are in the midst
of an epidemic of any disease, you are not necessarily suffering from the disease, but from the mesmerism of the public-
ity given the disease.

"The universal belief of good and evil operates hypnotically
upon any and every individual in this world. When you leave
your home in the morning, if you were to think it over you
would have to agree that you have no positive assurance that
you are going to get back at night. . . . Is there a way to avoid
this? Yes, there is, if those who are taught the principles could
break through their mental inertia in the morning to the extent
of consciously realizing:

There is but one power operating in this universe.
It is not a power of accident, death, disease, or sin.
There is only one power operating:
the same power that is causing the sun to rise on time
and to set on time, the same power that
is causing the tides to be in and out on time,
the same power that is bringing fish into the sea and

birds into the air. That is the power that
is operating in this universe, and that is the power
that is operating in my consciousness.
That is the law unto my experience.

There is no power in mesmeric suggestion
or statistics. There is no power in the belief
of infection and contagion. There is no power
in the carnal mind or in any of its forms or beliefs,
individual or collective.

"Watch to what degree the ordinary everyday mishaps stay outside your experience. 'A thousand shall fall at thy side, and ten thousand at thy right hand; but it shall not come nigh thy dwelling place.' Why? What is 'thy dwelling place'? It applies to the individual who dwells 'in the secret place of the most High,' not one who dwells in a house, in an automobile, or an airplane, but one who dwells 'in the secret place of the most High.'

"How can you do that? It has to be done consciously. Everything in your life is either an activity of your consciousness expressing itself or the result of your unwillingness to let your consciousness express itself, and thereby become a blotting paper for the beliefs of good and evil that permeate the world. You either become a blotting paper and take them all in and respond to them and show them forth, or you become master of your fate and captain of your soul—but only by an act of consciousness, not by saying, 'Oh, God will take care of it.' There must be an activity of truth in your consciousness, and that activity of truth has to be built. . . around the principle that there is only one power, that nothing but God and the activity of God is power, and that any sense of evil is impersonal and is nothing but the activity of the fleshly mind, the 'arm of flesh,' or nothingness.

"Every treatment has to be built around those principles. It makes no difference. . . what the nature of the human claim is.

It has to be consciously handled and every so-called treatment or realization must embody those principles. The one thing the world is suffering from is mental inertia. It will not wake up and think; it does not want to think conscious thoughts. It wants to look at pictures. It doesn't want to give voice to concrete truth. It doesn't want to sit back and live with truth. It wants to depend on an unknown God. . . .

"God is, and God is is-ing this very second. . . . There is no way for God to change. . . . Don't try to get God to be anything or do anything. God is. The responsibility is on your shoulders. . . . Wake up to the fact that your experience is going to be your own state of consciousness objectified. . . . If you insist on going around all day without living consciously in the realization of God, omnipresent, omnipotent, and omniscient here and now, the all and only power, and then impersonalizing all phases of evil and realizing that they exist only as the 'arm of flesh' or nothingness, you will not bring harmony into your experience.

"For a year this is difficult work and sometimes it may be a little longer than a year, but eventually something beautiful begins to happen. You don't have to consciously think; these things come to thought of their own accord. They automatically arise within you. . . . After that there is very little conscious effort. Now it all flows from within."

Joel S. Goldsmith, "Three Principles and Their Practice," *The 1959 Hawaiian Village Closed Class.*

Chapter Two

Letting the Seed
Take Root

Truth is not difficult to understand. As a matter of fact, it is very simple. That is why the Master said that children can receive it. "Verily I say unto you, Whosoever shall not receive the kingdom of God as a little child, he shall not enter therein."[1] Be as a little child, and you will be able to receive truth, but as an adult, or a mature person, you will find truth very difficult to receive.

Truth Is a Seed

You may hear or read a statement or a principle of truth and even recognize that this is the truth, and yet nothing happens to you. Reading statements of truth does not change anything, and you may think, "Why did I have to read that?" "Why did it seem true to me?" or "Why did it not do something for me?" That is because truth is a seed. Every truth heard or read that makes you feel it is truth, is a seed that is being taken into your consciousness. You can no more expect it to do something for you tomorrow than if you planted an apple seed today and expected to find apples growing in your yard tomorrow.

If you plant the seed of a tree, it may be months before you will see even the tiniest bit of green showing above the ground, and you could well wonder what was taking place all that time, but you know what was taking place. The seed broke open; the seed took root; the seed began to absorb food from the ground; and then suddenly that food was transformed into a shoot and appeared above the ground. If you are patient, it will become a bush, then a tree, and if you are still more patient, it will become blossoms, and then probably apples or peaches or pears.

So when truth touches your consciousness, do not think that you are now in heaven or that now that you have received this truth all the rest of your days are going to be spent in heaven on earth. No, you have merely had a seed of truth planted in your consciousness, and if you abide in that truth, if you let that seed abide in you, if you ponder it, it will come forth into full fruitage. If spiritual truth were just something intellectual like twelve times twelve is a hundred forty-four, then it could be that when you hear it once, it is yours forever. But because truth is spiritual, not intellectual, it must first be taken into the mind and there be nurtured, fed within, until eventually it comes forth as a realized or demonstrated truth.

Some truth might be given you now that years from now you will realize is the ultimate truth, but probably tomorrow, next week, or next month, you will wonder why it did not do something for you and later on you will have forgotten it entirely. It may be months or years before quite unexpectedly this truth will flow out of you and do miracles for you. You may say, "Why didn't that happen years ago when I first heard it?" The reason is that you probably heard it with your mind, and you may not yet have heard it with your inner ear, your spiritual ear.

Release God in God's Eternal Beingness

Every person can be healed of his discords very quickly if he will release God from any responsibility to heal him. Release God and acknowledge that you seek nothing of God, you desire nothing of God, you wish nothing of God. You release God because you understand that God made all that was made and all that God made is good. Anything that God did not make was never made. Whatever God did make is good. Therefore, you do not need God now: God's work was done in the beginning. You do not need God to correct Its mistakes. God has made no mistakes. You do not need God to heal you, for in the whole kingdom of God there is nothing to be healed.

Instead of living a life of duality, which is one of saying, "I am sick now. God, come to me and do something," live the life of single mindedness in which you realize:

Certainly, all that is, God made.
Anything that God did not make was not made;
therefore, it has no existence.
Since God looked upon all that He had made and
declared it to be good, there is no evil.
Therefore, I can release God from all
responsibility. I can release God and let Him go.

Do I not know that the sun will rise tomorrow?
Regardless of any clouds there may be in the sky to
hide it, the sun will rise.
I have released God and I am not going to
sit up tonight and pray God to bring
the sun up tomorrow. I know that God is about
God's business; therefore, the sun will rise.

I know the tides will come in and the tides will go
out, so I need not sit up tonight and pray that they
come in or that they go out. I will release God,
knowing that God is forever about His business. God
does not owe it to me to bring the tides in or out or
bring up the sun or set the sun. God is doing it as a
fulfillment of God's own being.

Our Work and Our Givingness, the Fulfillment of Our Nature

Some parents may have felt that they have done things for their children. But anything that parents have done is in the fulfillment of their own nature as parents. That is why they have done it. They fool themselves if they think that they have done it for any other reason.

When an artist paints a picture, he does not paint it for you, for me, or for the public. He is fulfilling his own nature. He may be disappointed if you and I do not appreciate it, but then he really did not paint it for you, me, or anyone else. It was the fulfillment of his nature. Anyone who has had experience with any form of art or literature of a creative nature knows that whatever he has done, he had to do as a fulfillment of himself, even though he would like to have others appreciate it. But even if they do not appreciate his work, he had to do it.

When you are quite honest with yourself, whatever you have done for your children, your neighbor, or in the way of philanthropy, charity, or benevolence, you have not in reality done it for the poor. You have done it as the fulfillment of your own nature.

God's Work, the Fulfillment of His Nature

God does nothing for you and God does nothing for me: God does everything as a fulfillment of the nature of God. He does not pick out only the good to do for. His rain falls "on the just and on the unjust."[2] His beauty is found in all countries; his grace is found among peoples of all races, religions, and in all varieties of everything. God is never doing anything for the white race or for the black race. God never does anything for Jews, for Protestants, or for Catholics. Whatever God is doing, He is doing as a fulfillment of His own being and He is doing it universally.

You benefit by this grace of God, not because God is picking you out or seeking you out to do good for, but because you are opening your consciousness to receive the grace of God which is forever flowing and which is forever on earth as it is in heaven. God is really fulfilling His own nature; He is fulfilling the fatherhood of God and the motherhood of God. God is the protective, maintaining, and sustaining influence, but God is also the loving and gentle influence; therefore, the fatherhood and motherhood of God are always being expressed.

When you and I accept that truth and stop thinking in terms of "God, do this for me or for mine," in other words, release God, loose Him, let Him go, and realize that the grace of God is as much yours as mine and as much mine as yours, then you will have entered into a whole new consciousness of life.

This is a high revelation, this ultimate revelation of the nature of God. But you would be surprised that, even though this seed is now planted within your consciousness, tomorrow or the day after you may not fully realize what has happened to you in knowing this truth. Nevertheless, one of these days you will wake up. You may not be thinking of this at all, and suddenly something will come into your thought, and you will know that God is love or God is life. You will not think of it just in connection with you, but will realize that this is a universal truth about God's nature and God's being.

Jesus' Work, the Fulfillment of His Nature

You may think of the great works of the Master and think that he did these works for you. He was not thinking of you. He was fulfilling his own nature. What he did he had to do as the fulfillment of that nature. He could not do less and there was not any more to do. He did it all. "Greater love hath no man than this, that a man lay down his life for his friends."[3] Sometimes we think that Jesus laid down his life for you or for me or for the Hebrews of his day. No, he had already discovered that most of them did not appreciate his message; most of them rejected it. He did not lay his life down for them. He laid his life down as a fulfillment of the vision within him that in losing his life, he was gaining it, and in giving of himself he was receiving the spirit of himself, the godliness of himself, the fulfillment of himself.

Specific Principles as Seeds: One Power

When you begin a study of the Infinite Way, you discover that there is somewhat of a system to it, that it is made up of specific principles, not one of which is original. In fact, there is no such thing as original truth, even the truth that was voiced by the Master. There was not a statement that he gave that was not known long before he was on earth. What there is, is truth which had not been accepted in consciousness or which had been accepted for a time and then had passed from the earth for one reason or another.

One of these principles with which you will work and which will be responsible for most of the good that comes into your experience will be the principle which we usually call "one power", but which sometimes we call "nonpower". Whether you read in the Infinite Way writings about one power or whether you read about nonpower, be assured that you are reading about the same thing. Nonpower and one power mean the same thing.

From Two Powers to Nonpower

One of these days this principle will come right back into your conscious awareness and produce miracles for you. In the human way of living, there are two powers. There is a power for good and a power for evil, just as the mind can be used for good purposes or for evil purposes, for unselfish or for selfish purposes. This is because in the human picture there are always the pairs of opposites. Some people use good power principally and other people use the power of evil principally, but the fact of the matter is that everyone uses the power of good sometimes and the power of evil at other times. No one is immune from the pairs of opposites in the human experience.

Electricity can be used to give light or cold or warmth. Electricity can also be used to kill. Airplanes are used for transportation, speed, and comfort, and airplanes are also used to kill. Even medicines which cure sometimes can kill. In the human picture, you are always dealing with two powers. When you come to a spiritual revelation, however, you will discover that the secret of the spirit is that there is only one power. That is why the Master could say to Pilate, who was the dictator of his day, "Thou couldest have no power at all against me, except it were given thee from above."[4] To the crippled, he could say, "Rise, take up thy bed, and walk."[5]

From Jesus' spiritual outlook, disease had no power. He did not ask God to heal the cripple. He proved that there was no power in that disease. If you read the four Gospels and follow the healings performed by Jesus, you will discover that he never once prayed to God to heal anybody; he never once asked God to do anything for anybody.

In every case, he just acknowledged that God is the only power and that this appearance he was facing was not a power at all. He faced every situation from the standpoint of one power, not from the standpoint of having God as a power over the power of sin or the power of disease or the power of lack. Even when he was feeding the multitudes, he did not pray to God for food. He just "took the five loaves, and the two fishes, and looking up to heaven, he blessed, and brake."[6] He did not acknowledge a power of lack; he never acknowledged a power of disease; he never acknowledged a power of sin; he did not ask God to heal anyone of sin. He just said, "Neither do I condemn thee."[7] In other words, there is no power in this.

Where Is Power?

You should face every situation in life from the standpoint that no situation has any power. Since God is the only power, disease can have no power, sin can have no power, fear can have no power: there is no power but God. "The kingdom of God is within you"[8]; therefore, all power and the only power there is, is within you. But do not make the mistake of trying to use it to heal, reform, or enrich anybody, because you will fail. Do not try to use God-power.

You will not find this teaching exemplified in the actual living conditions of our everyday world, whether you are dealing with a national condition, a weather condition, or a condition of health. In the Infinite Way, however, you are taught to face every situation with a realization that since God, the presence within you, is the only power, you need not fear what mortal man can do. You need not fear what mortal conditions can do or any mortal belief, because there is but one power, and it is within you. That power does not have to be used because if that is the only power there is, there is nothing on which to use it.

As you begin to look out at this world of appearances and remember all the appearances of evil that you can think about or have read about in the paper today, heard about on the air, or that you know about among your friends or family, try to remember the only reason these conditions persist is that persons believe they have power and they are trying, mistakenly, to exert a God-power to do something to that which has no power and which is no power. Then you will see how revolutionary this idea is in your own consciousness. You cannot at the moment even imagine the depth of this unfoldment, nor can you imagine the effect of it in your life when you begin to accept within yourself that out here there is no power:

> All power is within me, and it does not
> have to be used, because there is nothing out
> here on which to use it or use it against.

Even though you may agree with this principle and it may sound logical to you, and you may even feel good to know that there is no power against which to use God, nevertheless tomorrow, when you are facing the appearances of life, there will be that old temptation to reach out for God, to want God to do something to some evil. You have to train yourself to realize:

No, God, I released You last night.
You go ahead and fulfill Yourself.
You are about Your own business,
and I know that there is nothing in heaven or
on earth for which I need any power
that is not already functioning.
All the power that is necessary to bring up the sun
tomorrow is already operating;
all the power necessary to bring the tides in
and out is already at work.
All the power necessary to grow the crops or raise the
cattle is already functioning.

All the power necessary to maintain my life
is already at work, and all I have to do is
to acknowledge it. Acknowledge that God
is fulfilling Itself. God's nature is to fulfill Itself as
peace on earth and the divine grace in my life.
I do not pray for grace; I do not ask for grace:
I acknowledge grace as God's means of fulfilling Itself
on earth. God's means of fulfilling Itself
on earth is the power of grace.
When I acknowledge that and let myself be receptive,
I will find It functioning in my life.

Spiritual Power Not To Be Used

If you try to use God-power, if you try to make something happen, you are trying to play God. Let it happen; let God's grace, the activity of God, fulfill Itself; let God be the only presence and the only power; and do not believe these appearances out here which seem to need you to go around swinging a big stick, even a big spiritual stick.

Spiritual power is not a power over something. Spiritual power is the activity of God forever functioning. The moment you realize this and give up all attempts to use spiritual power, you will find that spiritual power is fulfilling itself in your experience. Spiritual power is not something you use; spiritual power is something you acknowledge to be the infinite presence and power of God on earth as it is in heaven.

The Principle of Omnipresence

Where is God? In no particular place. God cannot be limited to a place. God is infinite, eternal fulfillment, and the only answer to the question is that God is here, and it makes no difference whether that is being said in Sweden or in the United States, the North Pole or the South Pole. The only answer is, "The place whereon thou standest is holy ground,"⁹ because God is here. That is the only place where God is: here. Then if God is here, is there anything for you to do except to rest in that Word?

"In thy presence is fullness of joy."¹⁰ Where is God's presence? Here. Then right here is the "fullness of joy." Could there be fullness of joy if there were not fullness of health, fullness of supply, fullness of happy relationships, and fullness of all good? Of course not. Then right here is the fullness of spiritual peace and harmony and glory, not your glory or mine: God's glory, right here. Here is God's glory fulfilled, not by virtue of your praying for it but by virtue of God's nature to fulfill Itself here.

The Prayer of Acknowledgment

If there is any real prayer at all, it is the prayer of recognition, the prayer of acknowledgment and realization. Prayer is not asking anything of God and prayer is not expecting anything of God, because if there is any place where God is not expressed in Its fulness, there must be some place outside of God, which could not be if the nature of God is infinite being.

Infinite being includes all being and, therefore, here where you are, God is; here where he is, she is, or they are, God is. Should you then pray for God to do something or rather acknowledge that God's presence is the doing of it? Does God need to be reminded by you of what you need or what your family needs? Or are you to acknowledge that the omniscience of God—the all-wisdom—is the omnipotence of God—the all-power—in the omnipresence of God—the hereness and nowness of God. God is functioning. Is not that enough of a prayer? Lean not unto thine own understanding. In all thy ways acknowledge him, and he shall direct thy paths."[11] Do not tell God what you need or what your child needs. Do not tell God what your country needs.

Letting God Use You

"And thou shalt love the Lord thy God with all thine heart, and with all thy soul, and with all thy might."[12] How can you love God unless you understand God to be the all-wisdom, the all-power, and the all-presence? And then when you understand that here where you are God is, you rest. You rest. You do not tell God. You do not ask God. You do not expect something of God. You release God in the realization:

> God's presence is enough for me.
> His grace is sufficient for me.

That is not a prayer asking for anything or expecting anything. That is a statement of truth: "My grace is sufficient for there."[13] Then rest and let God's grace be made evident. The mind must come to rest. This principle is exemplified in the story of Hezekiah who, when his people told him the enemy was coming and that all the armies of the aliens outnumbered them, said, "With him is an arm of flesh; but with us is the Lord our God. . . . And the people rested themselves upon the words of Hezekiah."[14] This is important: they "rested" in his word. They did no more arguing; they did no more lighting of candles: they just rested in his word, and then the enemy fought among themselves and destroyed themselves while Hezekiah's people rested in his word.

Once you have acknowledged omnipresence, you have nothing more to do than to rest in the word. Loose God and let Him go. Release Him, and you will learn then that He has not lost or released you. Instead He has a firm grip on all that concerns you.

It is only when you are trying to use God or to use spiritual power that you lose the way. It is only when you start praying to God to tell God what you need, and probably what day you need it, that you lose the way. You begin to find God's grace when you release Him in the understanding that there can be only one power, and if there is only one power, spiritual power, why should you fear a material condition? Why should you fear a mental condition? Why should you fear a human condition of any kind if there is only one power? Then rest in that Word.

In some measure this principle will never leave you nor forsake you. You will never again be quite the same, but on the other hand you maybe surprised that it does not do what you think it should do. It should instantaneously wipe out of you all sin, disease, death, lack, and limitation, but the reason it does not do this is that it can do this for you only in proportion as you can spiritually feel it within you, not merely intellectually agree that it is true. That is merely a first and necessary step.

Unfolding Awareness

There is another step. Abide in God; be aware of God every day in whatever situation you face until you wake up. Students read and read, and it is all in the mind and has not yet registered. They have not heard it with their spiritual ears. Then one day all of a sudden it dawns on them, "Oh, God is love," and they go back and find that John said that two thousand years ago. But the force of the realization was so great that they may have thought it was completely original.

Many deep truths have come through me in the years that these books have been written, and yet sometimes it is two, three, or four years later that I have awakened and felt I had just discovered those truths, and then went back and found they were already in the books. Why? Because when they first came through, they were beautiful truths to me, but they were really only seeds planted in consciousness. It takes time for them to take root inside and later to come forth as a full blossoming tree of life. We all have that experience.

Some of the simplest truths that you are sure you know, someday you will discover that you never knew at all. They will come to you fresh as if you had never heard them. Then when you go back and find that you had known these truths all the time, you will say, "Why didn't I really know it? Look what it would have done for me!" But that is all right. It is part of your ongoing experience.

A New Generation

Unfortunately we were conceived and brought forth as separate and apart from God. The day is dawning when young couples are realizing, even when they marry, that they are not going to create children. They are just going to be the instruments through which God is going to send forth His children, and then they will accept their children, not as theirs but as gifts of God, full of the glory, the grace, and the beauty of God.

Such children will not grow up in fear of two powers. They will be brought up in the realization that there is only one power, only one presence, and they can go where they like because they never can escape from the presence of God. Then there will be a different generation of people. They will not be mortals who have to die and be reborn of the Spirit. They will be conceived and born of the Spirit to begin with.

That day is coming. We are witnessing it in youngsters who are just now being born; we are witnessing it in the case of young children who are being brought up by mothers who have learned this truth and are practicing it. We are witnessing the difference in those children—in their lives, in their health, in their intelligence, in their experience. We are seeing very remarkable things, not yet on a broad enough scale to say that the world has changed, but on a sufficiently broad scale to say we know now how it can be done and what the fruitage of it can be.

Before you expect to witness this change in your children or grandchildren, watch to what degree you can accept God as omniscience, the all-wisdom, the all-knowing, God as omnipotence, the only power, and therefore, a power that never needs to be used because there is no power on which to use it. It is the only power. Can you accept omnipresence to the point where you realize that even though you "walk through the valley of the shadow of death,"[15] God is there?

Overcoming the Fear of Death

Because of omnipresence, there is no place where God is not. Eventually when you really experience Paul's vision, "Neither death, nor life, . . . shall be able to separate us from the love of God,"[16] you will have overcome the fear of death. When you have overcome the fear of death you will have overcome death itself. Do not ever think that anyone overcomes death until he has overcome the fear of death, until he can agree within himself, "Living or dead, I'm still alive. Living or dead, I can never be separated from the love of God, so it is not important to me whether I'm alive or dead because dead or alive, I'm alive in God."

In that kind of overcoming, death has no power; there is then no sting in passing from human sight. By that time you realize that everyone has to pass from human sight at least to make room for someone else to come along. But passing from human sight is no longer a tragedy; passing from human sight is no longer a source of grieving.

Students who have not read the chapter, "Contemplation Develops the Beholder," in *The Contemplative Life* [17] will be shocked when they read the statement that there have been more troubles caused by birth than by death. We do not always like to think that, but it is true. So never think for a moment that it makes any difference to your daily experience, whether you are living in this country or that country, this side of the veil or that side of the veil, for when the veil is torn aside we will understand the scripture, "The darkness and the light are both alike to thee."[18] Never forget that. Darkness and light are not two different things: they are the same thing.

So, too, are life and death the same thing. They are just an infinite experience of unfolding God. This cannot be realized until you have realized that God is the only power and that God is the only power here, here wherever it is that you are—up or down, in or out, east or west, above or below—and here God is the only power. Relax in the recognition that God is the only power. You can look out at this world and can see the appearance of sin, disease, death, lack, and limitation and know that these cannot be true. "Let God be true, but every man a liar."[19] Let truth be true but every appearance a liar, for God is the only power and you can rest in that word.

Watch as you see how this truth grows in you day by day as a seed is growing, and then one day, the depth of its meaning dawns. Do not be surprised when it dawns if you are so completely aware of the astounding nature of it that you will forget that you ever heard it before and may even want to sit down and write a book about your new discovery.

Resting in I

Close your eyes and gently say, *I.* That *I* is your savior, your Christ, the son of God in you, the Father within.

I. I am that I Am. That I within me is the Father within me, and It is the substance of my life; It is the substance of my supply; It is the substance of my body; It is the substance of my health. As long as I can abide in that I that is within me, God is fulfilling Itself in my experience without my begging, without my pleading or entreating, just by relaxing. This I that is within me is mighty. This I that is within me is the source of my good twenty-four hours a day, asleep or awake.

As long as I live in the conscious realization of the presence of this I that is within me, this Father, this Son—for God, the Father, and God, the Son, are the same, One—as long as I abide in that realization, my good will ever unfold from within.

I have hidden manna, I have meat the world knows not of, and it is all embodied in the word I. I in the midst of me is the Father within me that does the works.

"He that seeth me seeth him that sent me," 20 for I and the Father are one, not two, just one. I and the Father are one, and that Father which I is, is the hidden manna, the pearl of great price, the meat that the world knows not of. This I in the midst of me is God, the Father, and God, the Son.

This I in the midst of me is bread, meat, wine, and water. This I that is within me is the resurrection, if necessary resurrecting me physically, mentally, morally, or financially. This I within me is God, the Father, and God, the Son, for they are one and therefore omnipresence. The presence of God is here where I am. God, the Father, is present where I am, for I and the Father are one. Then I can never be separated from the Father, I can never find myself in a place where the Father is not, for I and the Father are one—I, God, the Father, God, the Son, one, here where I am. Even in the midst of me is the hidden manna of life.

Chapter Three

Attaining the Christ-Mind

As students of the Infinite Way, you have a goal that must be attained. And there is a way to attain it. In order to understand this, I call your attention to a passage of scripture: "Let this mind be in you which was also in Christ Jesus."[1] That mind is not the ordinary human mind with which you think and reason. It is not that human level of mind at all. It must be a higher altitude of mind than the one used for mathematics, spelling, reading, and writing.

In Christian mysticism, that higher mind is referred to as the Christ-mind, Christ-consciousness, spiritual consciousness, or the fourth dimensional consciousness. All mysticism, whether Hebrew, Christian, or Oriental, has as its goal the attaining of that higher or fourth dimensional consciousness. It makes no difference whether your approach to the meaning of life is from an Oriental, Christian, or Hebrew standpoint, if you are approaching it from the mystical standpoint. It is all the same. When you attain the goal, you have some measure of that mind which was in Christ Jesus, the mind that does not see evil, the mind that does not judge.

What is "Righteous Judgment"?

From the standpoint of that Christ-mind, we are told to "judge not according to the appearance, but judge righteous judgment."[2] From the level of the human mind, if you see someone doing wrong according to your standards of wrong, you make it clear that it is wrong. But if you are seeing through the mind of the Christ, you would say, "Neither do I condemn thee.[3] . . . Who made me a judge or a divider over you?"[4] When you are seeing through the ordinary human mind, you wish to be avenged on those who harm you. But from the level of the mind of Christ, you say, "If you have taken my coat, you may have my vest also. If you have wronged me, I forgive you, and if you have wronged me twice, I forgive you twice, and if you have wronged me seventy times, I forgive you seventy times and seventy times seven times."

Spiritual Reliance

There is a different standard when you are living the life of a human being or when you have in some measure attained the Christ-mind. So, also, when you are operating out from the human mind, you live from the standpoint of your body. It is your heart that determines whether you live or die, or your stomach, muscles, or kidneys that determine whether you have health or disease. In your human state it is the body that determines whether you are sick or well and whether you live or die. In that state, it is the amount of money you have that determines whether you have a sufficiency or lack a sufficiency. You must count that money to be sure of what you can have and when you can have it, because as human beings you are living from the standpoint of money and of body.

When even a measure of the mind that was in Christ Jesus, the spiritual or unconditioned mind, is attained however, you will no longer take purse or scrip, nor will you take thought for your purse or scrip because your substance or supply is not in your pocketbook: it is in your soul. When you need something you do not take thought about your pocketbook. You turn within to your soul and then in due time whatever is necessary in the form of money will appear.

It is the same with health. You do not believe that you must breathe so many times to the minute; that you need so many vitamins or minerals, that your pulse must beat in a certain way, or that your blood must contain so much hemoglobin, because the mind that was in Christ Jesus does not have health in the body but in the soul. It does not take thought for what you shall eat or what you shall drink or wherewithal you shall be clothed. It does not take thought for your life, your heart, your liver, or your lungs.

The mind that was in Christ Jesus, the spiritual mind, which is a transparency, knows that your health, like your supply, is really of the substance of your soul or your consciousness. That is why in his day the Master was so little understood, and even less understood today when he said, "I am the resurrection and the life,"[5] not your heart, not your liver, not your lungs. "I am the bread of life,"[6] *I am* these, not money, but *I am:*

> I within my Soul have the substance of everything
> that I shall need in human affairs.

When there is a need to heal or feed the multitude, the Master looked up, meaning, he lifted himself above the pictures of sense; he looked above what the multitude saw and then he could command the disciples to break, share, give to everyone who was hungry. Out of the few loaves and fishes? Yes! Out of what you have, begin to share, and then discover that after everyone is fed there are twelve basketsful left over.

Begin with What You Have

You may think for a moment that you do not know enough

truth to help some friend or relative, but you have no right to judge by appearances because you should understand that no matter how much truth you know, of your own self you can do nothing. Therefore, you turn within and begin to use the little that you have, if it is only a few drops of oil. Even if you can remember only one passage from the Bible or one metaphysical statement, take that one into your consciousness: think of it; ponder it; meditate on it; repeat it; and it will multiply within you, and soon you will remember a second statement of truth or a second passage of scripture.

No one who is reading this Letter, who can begin with the one or two statements of truth he knows, would fail to find that he could go on for a whole hour giving a treatment. If necessary, it would flow and flow, and some of the things that would come he might say he had never realized he knew them or remembered that he had learned or read them years ago.

So it is that everyone who tries to have a tiny measure of that mind never stops to ask, "Can I do it? How can I do it? I do not know enough to do it." As the Hebrew master taught the widow, you begin with what you have in the house. If there is someone in need, and you have just one penny, share that one penny. Do not think that it is not enough. If that is what you can afford it is enough. The Master said that the mite of the widow, which was the widow's all, was enough. It would not have been enough if a millionaire had given it, but it was enough because it was her all.

Whether it is with money or whether it is giving help, comfort, or healing to somebody, do not stop to ask yourself how much you have. Begin with what you know you have: one statement of truth, one Biblical passage. Begin to ponder it; meditate on it; bless it; realize this truth about the person you wish to help, and continue pondering for five, ten, or fifteen minutes. You will see how truth multiplies within you and then you will understand that our object or goal in the Infinite Way is to attain that mind which does not judge by appearances or by human standards and which does not live by bread alone.

The Bread and Meat Within

"Man shall not live by bread alone, but by every word that proceedeth out of the mouth of God."[7] Man shall not live by breath alone; man shall not live by lungs alone; man shall not live by heart alone; man shall not live by muscles alone; man shall not live by years alone; man shall not live by youth alone; man shall not live by money alone; but "by every word that proceedeth out of the mouth of God." As you remember this each day, you are developing in you the mind that was in Christ Jesus. Every time you resist the temptation to think that you live by bread alone or heart alone, every time you resist the temptation to believe that you live by anything in the world of effect, you are lifting yourself out of humanhood, out of the human mind and human limitations, and you are beginning to live out from the Spirit as the Master did.

Of course, Jesus was not understood when he told the woman of Samaria that he could give her water even without a bucket. In the materialistic human life the only kind of water known is the kind that can be poured out of buckets or bottles. The human being does not know of the water that is stored up inside, which is the water of life, the spiritual word of God. Only with the mind "which was. . . in Christ Jesus" can it be known.

Think of how shocked the disciples were when they noticed the Master had not eaten, and he said, "I have meat to eat that ye know not of."[8] Where was this meat? It was not in his hand, and they knew it was not in his pocket. Where was it? It was the word of God which was his meat and drink. "My meat is to do the will of him that sent me, and to finish his work."[9]

Dwelling in "the Secret Place"

The Infinite Way is a transcendental or mystical teaching

because it is not human, it is not material, it is not mortal: it is a revelation of a depth of consciousness that each one has, but which lies deep within. The Master called it "the kingdom of God. . . within you." [10] This kingdom of God is the mystical realm which is not to be found "Lo here! or, Lo there! for, behold, the kingdom of God is within you." [10] In the human world we seek outside for our good. In the spiritual realm we learn that the kingdom of God is within.

> *I*, within you, *I* in the midst of you am mighty.
> *I* am your bread, your wine, and your water.
> *I* am your drink, your food, and your health,
> your harmony, your completeness, your perfection.

Once you perceive this and begin to understand it, you will understand why "the place whereon thou standest is holy ground," [11] and you will "put not your trust in princes, nor in the son of man, in whom there is no help." [12] You "will not fear what mortal man shall do." [13] Why? "They that take the sword shall perish by the sword." [14] You are living not by the sword and not by bread, but by every word of God that is stored up in your consciousness.

Every word of God that you can draw forth from your consciousness is your daily bread, your health, your happiness, your prosperity, your safety, and your security. The Ninety-First Psalm reveals that if you dwell "in the secret place of the most High. . . there shall no evil befall thee, neither shall any plague come nigh thy dwelling." [15] But if you are living through the human mind that tries to find health in the body, life in the heart, supply in the pocketbook, you are not living "in the secret place of the most High." You are living in your body or you are living in your pocketbook.

You are living the mystical life only when you begin to live in this "secret place of the most High" and realize that the kingdom of God is within you. You are not thinking of the person on your left or your right. You are not expecting anything of your husband, wife, your parents, or your children. You are living within your own being.

> The storehouse of God is within me,
> and I am not dependent on
> "man, whose breath is in his nostrils." [16]

Cease from depending on man if you would enter the kingdom of God, the mystical realm where God is your life, your high tower, your rock, and your foundation.

Spiritual Vision, Necessary to Live the Mystical Life

There is a human sense of life which is completely one of limitation, one that is wholly dependent on how many dollars you have or on how many times your heart beats to the minute. In that human sense of life, you are dependent on the men and the women in your life. But if you are to obey the Master, it is necessary that you come out and be separate, that you have in you "that mind which was also in Christ Jesus," and know what you mean when you say that. Have in you that mind that does not hold one in condemnation to his past, that mind in you which is willing to forgive the present and the future, that mind in you which is ready at any moment to share the bread of life, that mind in you which is ready to comfort, to heal, to save, to redeem.

This is the fourth dimensional life, the transcendental life, the life of spiritual consciousness, and it begins in that moment when you agree that your life is Self-sustained, Self-maintained, when you agree that you are not living by what the body tells you, but by what you learn from the word of God that is revealed within you.

In any moment of your life, you can begin the ascent; you can begin the journey back to the Father's house. In your human sense of life, you are a prodigal son. Each day you are using up some of your life and you have only enough to last until threescore years and ten or twenty. Each day some of your strength, health, or wisdom is lessening in the human picture. That is the life of the prodigal.

The moment that you realize, "Man shall not live by bread alone" or by the body, but by every word that proceeds out of the mouth of God, you are not living on your strength, your supply, your body, or the number of your years. Now you are drawing forth your life and abundance from the source. It is not different from a lake which, cut off from a river, would dry up eventually and there would be nothing left. Only when a lake is attached or is at-one with the river can it use up any amount of water all day long, because more is always pouring in from its source, the river.

The Master revealed this truth in his illustration of the branches of a tree. If you are a separate branch out in the world, you are using yourself up, and eventually you will come to where the Prodigal Son came. But if you are realizing that you are being fed by those immortal, eternal waters of life within you and sustained by the meat, the wine, the water, and the bread of spiritual life, then day by day you are renewed and no matter what you give away, no matter what you use up, it is instantly renewed and supplied to you again so that there is no such thing as being depleted or running down.

It takes a measure of spiritual vision for a person to be aware that he is not living by bread alone, that he is not depending on "man, whose breath is in his nostrils," that he is not judging by how many years have gone over his head, or by the testimony of the heart, liver, or lungs. The reward is that he finds that his life is lived by every word of God that is in his consciousness, every word of God that he can remember, ponder, and meditate upon.

The Omnipresence of All Good

One reason you and I are in the Infinite Way is that we may rise above the limitations of the human mind and attain some measure of "that mind which was also in Christ Jesus." Already I have shown you part of the way of attaining it. First of all, make the decision: Am I going to or do I want to continue to judge my life by what my heart, my pocketbook, or my birth date tells me? Do I want to judge by appearances or do I want the kingdom of God that is within me and live by every word that proceeds out of the mouth of God?

Then must come the ability each day not to make judgments on the basis of your own limitations. You will soon discover that even if this were your first day in spiritual living you would have infinity. Why? Because you have nothing of yourself and you have all that is God's.

When the Father says, "Son, thou art ever with me, and all that I have is thine,"[17] He is not speaking just to James, William, Robert, Mary, or Sue. He is speaking to every individual on the entire globe: those who have passed on, those who are here, and those who have not yet been born. No one can escape from God's infinite allness. It was Paul who gave us that principle in one statement: "Neither death, nor life. . . shall be able to separate us from the love of God,"[18] from the care and infinite supply of God.

All those who have gone on before us have the infinite allness of God; and those not yet born will have the infinite allness of God when they arrive here. Unfortunately parents do not teach this to their children when they are born. Too bad that they did not know this truth. It is too bad also that Jesus did not know about airplanes in his day. He could have covered a bigger territory in spreading the gospel of truth. As it was, he was limited to the distance he could walk, and so it has taken a long time for his words to reach out around the world. Nevertheless he could have had an airplane. The laws of aerodynamics were already there. God did not invent the airplane in this generation. The laws governing the airplane always existed, only awaiting man's discovery.

Releasing Infinity

The infinite abundance of God has always been in every individual who ever existed, but he could not demonstrate it until someone could come along and reveal that within him is the kingdom of God, within him is all that the Father has. All the music is there, all the art, all the literature, all the spiritual truth, all the inventions, all the sciences. All these are within, but to experience them a person must begin to open out a way for the infinity of God to escape. Truth is within. The truth, which is bread, meat, wine, and water, is not to be found outside, but is within, and a way must be found for "the imprisoned splendor" to escape. Begin to pour now. There is no better way to begin to pour than to set aside periods each day to pray for those whom you know need prayers, those within your family, your community, within your nation, and eventually within the entire world.

Begin to pray the prayer of forgiveness, "Father, forgive them; for they know not what they do."[19] Release everyone from condemnation and punishment. Know every bit of spiritual truth you can about all those who are within your consciousness. Know that the voice is saying to them, "Son, all that I have is thine. . . . Neither death, nor life. . . can separate you from the love and care of God." This is giving. You are sharing out of that infinite storehouse; you are pouring out the water of life even without a bucket. Through such meditation, you are developing more and more of that spiritual or fourth dimensional transcendental consciousness.

Attaining the Fourth Dimensional Consciousness

The many ways that have been revealed to me of attaining the fourth dimensional consciousness are incorporated in the writings. Those wishing to make a real study of this should begin with *Living the Infinite Way.*[20] In this book certain principles are presented and clarified. Follow this book with *Practicing the Presence*[21] and after that book comes *The Art of Meditation*.[22] Why this sequence? Meditation is not easy. In fact, meditation is very difficult for those who have not attained this ability, because meditation is reaching an inner stillness so that you do not have to think thoughts. In that inner silence, you can hear the voice of God; you can hear those words of truth that pour forth from within you. You do not address God: you hear God. You receive impressions from within.

To many people this is not simple. It was revealed to me, and practice has proven, that if we begin with practicing the presence of God, it leads to an inner stillness that makes it possible to meditate. Using the book *Practicing the Presence,* you can begin to practice the presence. How? The very moment that your eyes open from sleep, before you are out of bed, pause for a moment to remember:

This is God's day.
God gave me this day:
I didn't. I just woke up and found it already here.
But the process of turning night into day is
an activity of God and, therefore, this day to which
I am awakening is God's day.

God is in this day and God is in everyone
on this earth or off this earth, for God is everywhere.
God fills all space. God governs this day;
God governs every individual in this day;
God governs the circumstances of life in this day.

In other words, with your first waking thought, you acknowledge the presence of God, the activity of God, the government of God, the love of God. When you have done that, you can get up and take care of your physical preparations for the day.

Acknowledge God as the Source

The moment you turn to your breakfast, you must pause for the practice of the presence and acknowledge that it is the grace of God that sets the food on your table. Somebody one time thought he was being very humorous to say, "Ah, yes, and the money I earn." But he was very limited in his perspective because money does not produce food. All the money that was ever printed or minted will not grow a single acre of wheat. It takes God to do that; it takes the laws of nature to do that. Separate those laws of nature from the earth, and you can have all the money in all the mints in the world and starve. You will then discover how true it is that there was food on the earth before money was invented. In fact, there was food on the earth before there was a man to eat it.

All that man has ever needed was in the earth when he arrived here. The oil that we use for gasoline was in this earth thousands of years before the automobile was thought of. The gold and the silver governments fight for was here before there were governments to misuse them. So every time you eat, whether it is twice a day, three times a day, or four times a day, first acknowledge that it is the grace of God that produces the food in the earth, the waters, or the air above the earth, the grace of God. Then you are practicing the presence of God.

When you leave your home for your office or your market, be sure that you pause again to remember that the presence of God goes before you to "make the crooked places straight."[23] You know from reading your newspapers of the things that are happening in the lives of those who are satisfied to go out into the world, thinking that they themselves can bring themselves safely home. No, only the grace of God establishes you in your way. Therefore, never leave home without a conscious remembrance that there is a presence within you that goes before you to "make the crooked places straight,"[23] to prepare "mansions"[24] for you.

After three or four weeks of this practice, an inner stillness will have developed in you. You will no longer be living separate from God, no longer living unto yourself. Three or four weeks of this practice and you will feel, "Why, God has been here all the time. It is I who have neglected God, not God who has neglected me." When you feel this stillness, this inner peace that comes with the constant remembrance of God, then when you sit down to meditate, your thoughts will not wander all over the place. You will be able to sit down and almost immediately be in a receptive attitude with your ears open. Then meditation will come quickly to you, and if you need any guide or help, you will find it in *The Art of Meditation.*

The Purpose of Spiritual Healing

By this time you should be having some experiences of a healing nature, which will lead you to the book *The Art of Spiritual Healing.* [25] After that, it does not make any difference in what order you read or study the books because in every one of them you will find the specific principles repeated in many different ways.

When you come to the healing work, whether for yourself, your family, or for others, you will discover that in the Infinite Way there are healing principles, which are not to be found in any other metaphysical teaching. These are specific principles which have revealed themselves to me, and these principles constitute one reason that the Infinite Way in a relatively short time has spread to five continents. This has been accomplished without an organization, without memberships, without dues, without asking anyone for financial support. It has spread purely by the power of the word that is within the message, that is, by virtue of the healings. This includes not only specific healings of mental, physical, moral, and financial ills, but that broader base of healing, which is the renewal of man, the rebirth, the putting off of that human mind with its limitations and putting on immortality, revealing the mind that was in Christ Jesus, which enables a person to live differently and by different standards than before. Thus he is at peace, not only with God, not only with himself and his family, but with the community. These principles are now operating far beyond the level of merely individual healing.

These principles are being used by some persons in commercial and governmental affairs. The basis of such work is that evil, regardless of its name or nature, is not personal. It is not a person's thinking that has produced his troubles; it is not the ignorance or the sin or the fear in him. It is not anything of any nature in a person that is responsible for the evils that he meets, nor is it the evils of this world that prevent his business from prospering, nor is it because the world is at war or at peace. In other words, business is as independent of the times as health is independent of a person's body.

Your health is not dependent on your body, and your supply or your business is not dependent on the country in which it is located, or whether it is a boom time or a time of panic, a peace time or war time. Your life and your business and your harmony are embodied in your soul, and the evils that have beset you are equally impersonal. From the moment that you recognize this, they begin to disappear out of your experience. Heretofore, when you have thought there was some fault in you responsible for your troubles, or if you blamed one of your friends or relatives, you were personalizing and you were perpetuating your troubles.

It Is Your Responsibility

When you begin to catch the principles of the Infinite Way and apply them and stop malpracticing yourself and your neighbor, and begin to understand that all evil is absolutely impersonal and impotent because it is not of God, you will begin to understand the healing principles that will begin to operate instantly in you and for you.

But how are these principles going to affect the people in your business who know nothing about this and how will it affect your customers or clients? They do not have to know anything about these principles. What is necessary is that you know that whatever has operated as a negative influence in your experience is impersonal and impotent because it is not of God, and immediately you will watch and see how the discords and even the discordant persons begin to disappear from your experience. Some of them will no longer be a problem either because of being healed or by being removed, but not by virtue of your treating them, not by virtue of your malpracticing them, but by your ignoring those ungodlike traits through knowing these specific principles.

Your practitioner can help you through any kind of an emergency, but your practitioner cannot take you into heaven. That is something you have to do by knowing the truth. The Master said, "Ye shall know the truth, and the truth shall make you free."[26] He did not say, "I will know the truth and make you free." He said, "Ye shall know the truth." Remember that scene at Jerusalem which should be etched in the mind of every person. Can you not see Jesus with his arms outstretched, "O Jerusalem, Jerusalem, thou that killest the prophets, and stonest them which are sent unto thee, how often would I have gathered thy children together, even as a hen gathereth her chickens under her wings, and ye would not!"[27] They were satisfied to sit there and let him heal them. They were satisfied to sit there and let him feed them, but they wanted to come back again to be healed and fed tomorrow and the day after tomorrow. That is not the way of spiritual living.

Spiritual living is to know the truth, "and the truth shall make you free." The responsibility is up to you, once the Father has awakened in you a desire for truth, a desire to know God. From then on it is you who must find your way back to God through study, meditation, and practice. In the degree that you take the couple of drops of spiritual oil that you have and let them pour out of you by forgiving and loving more, you discover the great secret which the Master has embodied in two great passages: "Inasmuch as ye have done it unto one of the least of these my brethren, ye have done it unto me. . . . Inasmuch as ye did it not to one of the least of these ye did it not to me."[28]

Whatever you do of good to another you have done to yourself. Whatever of good you have not done to another you have not done to yourself.

Chapter Four

The Temple

Spiritual teaching involves an emptying out of the old "bot-tles"[1] to make way for the new wine. You cannot fill a vessel already full. You cannot receive a spiritual impartation in a mind filled with universal beliefs, theories, or opinions. Concepts and misconceptions must be cleared out of the mind so that it can become a transparency for truth. Mind is not a power. Mind has no power for good or for evil. Mind is a receiving and a transmitting instrument.

To understand the mind, first look at your body and realize that this body is your body, and that you can do with your body what you will. If you choose to walk to the right, your body has no power to resist you and walk downstairs. Your body has no power of its own. Your body cannot be moral or immoral; your hands cannot be honest or dishonest. Your body has no qualities of its own. It is merely a mechanical instrument fashioned for your use.

Now go a step further and see that just as you have a body, so, too, you have a mind. You can use your mind to develop a talent, a profession, or a business. It is your mind, and you can educate it in mathematics, music, art, science, or literature. You can keep your mind imbued with truth by filling it with scripture, spiritual and inspirational writings, or mystical poetry. You can keep your mind filled with truth or you can keep your mind filled with trash. You determine how many hours a day worthwhile literature is poured into your mind. You have the capacity to determine the nature of what goes into your mind. Just as your body is not a power unto itself, so your mind, also, is not a power. It cannot talk back to you; it has no control over you: you have control over it.

When a person no longer has control over his mind and his mind appears to run away with him, he is labeled insane. The truth is that it is his mind. He has the power to govern, instruct, and educate it.

The Human Mind
Is Conditioned by False Knowledge

When the mind is filled with misconceptions or false knowledge, it creates an inner chaos, disorder, or sense of limitation. Before 1492, when the mind of man was convinced that the earth was flat, that the sky sat on the horizon, and that ships could not travel beyond the boundaries circumscribed by universal ignorance or they would fall off the earth, that misinformation limited the entire universe to the particular continent on which men found themselves.

But when Christopher Columbus sailed to North America, he proved that the earth was round, and the limitations of the belief in a flat earth fell away from mankind. Big ships were built that sailed the high seas, bringing treasures from one part of the world to the other, resulting in intercontinental merchandising and also an intercontinental exchange of art, literature, and science. All this became possible because a misconception of the mind was corrected, and the truth about the shape of the earth was revealed.

It might be said that the mind had power over those people who were limited by their concepts. The mind had nothing to do with it: it was the misinformation in the mind, because the mind had taken in whatever it was fed.

If we are fed with misconceptions about God so that we have no knowledge of the nature of God, and if we pray to God to send us a ton of coal and it does not arrive, we cannot blame the mind. We have fed the mind with that misconception about God and about prayer. Think of all the misconceptions that the religious world has entertained for centuries, and then you will understand how much clearing out of these misconceptions must take place before the mind is unconditioned and ready to receive truth.

The Mind, a Receptive Instrument

In this present century, many persons have mistak~ ~ been taught that mind and thought are power with that they have come to fear the mind and to fe~ ~ not only fear the thoughts of other perso~ ~ they fear their own, all because of a mistak~ ~ that thought is power and that mind is power.

In the early days of such teachings, remarkable demonstrations took place. These demonstrations, however, were merely exchanging one belief for another. Mind and thought are not power except in the degree that those who accept erroneous beliefs, such as the idea that the world is flat, limit themselves by their beliefs. In that way thought or mind has power to restrict a person. But really it is not mind or thought: it is the misconceptions or false teachings that are fed into the mind. The mind at all times is prepared to receive truth if it is fed with truth, just as the mind is prepared to receive a lie. The mind is ready at any time to accept what you feed it: a false belief, a false appetite, a false teaching. The mind cannot resist what you pour into it. It is merely an instrument.

If you pour a good quality of lubricating oil into the motor of your car, it must accept it, just as if you pour an inferior quality of oil into your car it must accept that. The motor is merely an instrument that has no power to think, agree, or disagree. It must accept what you put into it.

At one time a large computer was giving out incorrect information. This was because it had no power to do anything else. It had to give out what had been poured into it. If you put the cogs or wheels in the wrong place, they will of course act imperfectly. It is not the computer giving wrong information; it is the wrong adjustment of the computer.

Your mind is a transparency. It will reflect back to you what you pour into it. Many of you have proved in a measure that if you sit in the silence in meditation or treatment, pouring into yourself the realization that God is infinite, God is spirit, God is omnipresent, God is omnipotent, God is omniscient, only God is law, only God is life, and there is no power apart from God, spirit, soul, you witness harmony come into your experience or into the experience of your patients or students. In the degree that you have poured truth into your mind, in that degree has harmony come into the outer world.

On the other hand, what is entering the lives of those who sit all day long pouring into their minds the typical television program, with sensational newspaper stories and blaring radio programs sandwiched in between? God, spirit, soul, purity, integrity? Of course not. They are filling their mind with the negative things of life, and that is all that the mind can give back to them.

The Real Goal

If you study the Infinite Way writings and the tape recordings until you receive a higher unfoldment as to the nature of God and prayer or until you have washed out of the "bottle" some of the old concepts of God and prayer, so that your mind is unconditioned, then you are ready for the revelation of the mystical approach to life, which is what you who come to this path should be seeking. You are not seeking merely to change bad health into good health, or lack into abundance. As you exchange your ignorance of God or your sense of separation from God for an awareness, an actual experience of God's presence, watch the illness, the lack, and the unhappiness drop away.

The so-called good things of life are the added things. They are not the goal. The goal is God-realization; the goal is the God-experience; the goal is the demonstration of the presence of God in the midst of you. If you make that your goal and if you realize that whatever you pour into your mind or body will determine its nature, then you will begin to see how harmony is brought into your existence, how because of this inflow of spirit you are enabled to impart some measure of that spirit to others in the degree of their receptivity, and ultimately witness the Pentecostal experience as it descends upon the entire world.

The Master said, "My kingdom is not of this world.[2] . . . Peace I leave with you, my peace I give unto you: not as the world giveth, give I unto you."[3] He also said, "Take no thought for your life, what ye shall eat, or what ye shall drink; nor yet for your body, what ye shall put on.[4] . . . Which of you by taking thought can add one cubit unto his stature?"[5] So you are to take no thought now for what you eat, drink, or wherewithal you are clothed or transported. You are to take no thought for your life. You are to take no thought for a demonstration of an added inch to your height, or a ten-pound weight loss or gain. You are to take no thought for any human demonstration. What are you to do? "Seek ye first the kingdom of God, and his righteousness."[6] That is what you are to do. That is your goal, knowing full well what comes next: "all these things shall be added unto you."[6]

How to Find the Kingdom of God

In what way do you seek the kingdom of God? First of all, it is necessary to find out where this kingdom is that you are seeking. The Master gave the answer to that, too. "Neither shall they say, Lo here! or, Lo there! for, behold, the kingdom of God is within you."[7] Then how shall you seek this kingdom that is within you? Be still. In quietness and in confidence. Not by might or by power. You cannot take heaven by storm.

The kingdom of God that you are searching for is within you, and the God that you are seeking is in the "still small voice."[8] "He uttered his voice, the earth melted."[9] Now you have the entire secret of the spiritual life. It remains only for you to demonstrate and experience it. And you have a far greater opportunity to experience it since you know what goal you are seeking, where the kingdom of God is and how God is to be found.

It is necessary, also, to clear out a great deal of rubbish from your mental household. Heretofore you have been told, first of all, that before you can hope to experience God you must be good, you must be deserving, you must be spiritual, you must be baptized or have communion. But now it is revealed that whether you live in an age where there are churches or no churches, rituals or no rituals, God is available as long as those who are seeking God are seeking It within themselves.

Invite God

There is no call upon you to do anything outwardly to find God because God is within you and God is known to you through the still small voice. This is not dependent on any wisdom or on any action of yours. It is dependent on the grace of God. There is nothing you can do externally to bring God to you, nor is there anything you can do to prevent God coming to you if you fulfill the qualifications for that essential inner receptivity.

It is done by an inner stillness and an opening of the inner ear. Be still. In quietness and confidence, listen for the still small voice. Invite God to speak. Invite God to reveal Itself and then be sure to have enough quiet periods during the day, even if each one is only one, two, or three minutes, so that you are making room for that "imprisoned splendor to escape."[10] Remember, God is not coming to you from outside. The imprisoned splendor is locked up within you, and you must open out a way for it to escape. You must invite God to speak from within you.

Let I Raise You Up

By your listening ear, develop a pathway from your ear deep inside your consciousness, always listening, always expectant. Even when you are about your day's work, there is no reason you cannot keep a line open down into your consciousness and remind yourself, "Speak, Lord; for thy servant heareth."[11] Then one day It will speak, and you will hear It say, "Be still, and know that I am God."[12] From that moment, you are on a rung of the ladder leading upward to the God-experience. In fact, you have already tasted in a mild way the first experience of God when you either hear or feel within you, "Be still, and know that I am God," because with this, the opening up of the entire secret of Christ Jesus comes to you. This was the secret he gave to the world, a secret I will repeat to you now:

> *I* in the midst of me, the *I* deep down
> within me is God. Let me be still and know that
> *I* in the midst of me is God.

From that moment on, all the rest of the Master's teaching unfolds.

> *I* will never leave you. *I,* God, *I,* Christ, the son of
> God, the spirit of God in you, will never leave you or
> forsake you. Fear not, *I* am with you.

And if out here there seems to be a lack of any nature, listen, and you will hear, "*I* have meat the world knows not of.

Relax and rest. *I,* in the midst of you, *I* have meat." As you rest and relax from effort, struggle, and strife, that which appeared to be lacking soon makes its appearance in your life.

If you are faced with an appearance of discord of any kind, as you learn to be still and know that *I* am God; you will hear It: "I am come that you might have life and that you might have life more abundantly." Immediately a weight drops away from your shoulders and you let this "imprisoned splendor" escape. It will go before you to "make the crooked places straight."[13] It will appear outwardly as the substance of your food, clothing, housing, and transportation. These will be the things added after you have heard the voice of God:

> *I* am the meat; *I* am the resurrection.
> If for any reason any part of your life has been
> destroyed, *I* in the midst of you will resurrect it,
> for *I* am the resurrection. Relax and let
> *My* presence rise in you and raise you up.
> For *I,* if *I* be lifted up in you, will raise you unto *Me.*
> *I* will lift you out of the tomb: the tomb of sick flesh,
> the tomb of misery, the tomb of loneliness. *I* in the
> midst of you, if *I* be raised up in you, if you
> recognize *I* in the midst of you, *I* will raise you up,
> and *I* will raise up your purse and your business.
>
> *My* presence goes before you;
> *My* presence walks beside you; *My* peace *I* give unto
> you: *My* peace, spiritual peace, Christ-peace.

If you are seeking the peace that the world can give, you cannot receive the spiritual peace that leads to the added things out here. It must be only *My* peace that you are seeking. It must be only the Christ-peace, the spiritual peace, that the world cannot give, and when you receive it, those other things of the world are added unto you, not by mentally creating them; but by letting the spirit of God in you come forth. You have raised up the *I*, the Christ, in you, and in raising up that Christ in you, It has raised you up unto Its level, out of your humanhood into your divinity.

It is important that you learn to ignore the appearances temporarily so that you do not fight them, battle them, or try to overcome them. Ignore them while you go inside and hear the still small voice as it reassures you, "This is my beloved Son, in whom I am well pleased."[14] Do you need to hear any more than that? Do you need to see signs and wonders? Do you need anything more than a simple assurance given within, "Son, thou art ever with me, and all that I have is thine"[15]? Is it not possible then to relax and rest in the assurance of the divine presence within?

The Omnipresence of the Christ

It has been taught that the Christ lived two thousand years ago, walked the Holy Land, was crucified, buried, resurrected, and ascended up to heaven. Ever since then the Christian world has been waiting for the Christ to come again. But this Christ that lived two thousand years ago and manifested through Christ Jesus, lived three thousand years ago, and manifested through Moses, Isaiah, Elijah, Elisha, and dozens of others. This same Christ never was crucified, never was buried, never was resurrected, never ascended up to heaven.

This Christ is incarnate in you and in every individual who has ever been born since time began, whether he was born in occidental, oriental, pagan, or aboriginal countries. Wherever an individual has been born, the Christ has been incarnate in him: the hidden priceless pearl, the hidden manna, the secret word. It is just as much in you as It ever was in any prophet, saint, or seer of old, and in the same degree—not a little bit of it. You cannot divide spirit. Spirit is incorporeal, and It is in you. The kingdom of God is in you. The Christ that dwelt in Paul dwells in you.

Until you stop believing that the Christ was crucified, until you stop believing that the Christ left this earth and may come again, you will not be able to accept the absolute presence of that Christ or son of God within you. And it is necessary to do so. If you would be on the spiritual path, you must accept the truth that the *I* will never leave you or forsake you, and that that *I* is the Christ speaking through Jesus and saying, "I will never leave thee, nor forsake thee."[16] Therefore, the Christ dwells in you.

The Christ, the Multiplier and the Healer

If you can accept this, you can go on to the next step and ask, "What is the function of this Christ in me?" And then go back to the Master who explained what the Christ-function was in him, because what the Christ-function was in him, the Christ-function is in you: to heal the sick, to raise the dead, to feed the hungry, to forgive the sinner, to preach the gospel. This is the function of the Christ in you. It is to teach you this truth.

If you will develop an inner stillness, so that you can learn to hear the still small voice, the Christ will preach to you. It will reveal this truth to you. It will reveal Its message with signs following. It will lift you up and reveal to you your eternal life. *I* am come. This Christ in the midst of you is come that you might have life and that you might have it more abundantly. *I Am,* this Christ, is your bread, meat, wine, and water. This Christ in the midst of you is the resurrection of your body, your business, your home, the resurrection of everything you believe you may have lost. The function of the Christ in you is to raise you up to Its own level: *I,* if *I* be lifted up in you, will lift you unto *Me.*

The function of the Christ is to multiply: to multiply the loaves and fishes, to multiply everything in your experience that needs multiplying. It is not my function or yours to multiply: it is the function of the Christ in you. Your acknowledgment of this and your realization of this lets the Christ perform Its function of multiplication.

Whatever the Master did two thousand years ago was the direct action of the Christ or the Father within him. Everything he did, everything of that nature, must be done by the Father within or the indwelling Christ today the same as two thousand years ago or else there would be no truth to the scripture that says that God is the same from everlasting to everlasting: yesterday, today, and forever. God is the same; God changes not. Therefore the function of God in the Master is the function of God in you.

The Body, the Temple of Consciousness

Another misconception to be wiped away is that you were conceived in sin and brought forth in iniquity. But you are to "call no man your father upon the earth: for one is your Father, which is in heaven,"[17] one Creator, and that is God. Therefore you are the offspring of God. That is not the offspring of sin. The longer you look upon yourself as a mortal or as a human being with traits of inheritance, or the longer you look upon yourself as conceived in iniquity and brought forth in sin, the longer you prevent your own demonstration as the temple of God.

"Know ye not that ye are the temple of God?[18] . . . Know ye not that your body is the temple of the Holy Ghost which is in you?"[19] What is the use of playing around with those outworn theological misconceptions when you have a divinely inspired piece of scripture to tell you that you are the temple of God? And this must be so if the kingdom of God is within you. Then you are the temple in which that God functions, the temple not made with hands.

Here is the mystery. You look at yourself in the mirror, and you see what seems to be a corporeal body and immediately identify this with yourself, whereas this body is not you: this body is yours. You are incorporeal and spiritual. You are not in this body. You never have been inside this body. You never have looked out from within this body. Surgeons can look from head to foot and cannot find you in the body. They never will. You are not in this body. And this body is not you.

> This body is mine. Where am I?
> If I look up and down from head to foot,
> I will not find me. I am not here. I am risen.
> I am not in any tomb. I am not in any corporeality.
> I am not in any tomb of body or matter.
> I am risen; I am spirit; I am the temple of God.
> "I and my Father are one," [20] and I am always in my
> Father and my Father is in me.
> That has nothing to do with this body.

> This body is my trolley-car, my automobile, that I
> use with which to get around, a mechanical function.
> But it is not I. I am not a piece of mechanism. I am
> the instrument of God, the transparency for God, the
> offspring of God. I am the temple of God, and I am
> in my Father, and my Father, is in me, for we are
> one. God is not corporeal, and I am not corporeal;
> God is not physical, and I am not physical.

I *Is the Password to Fulfillment*

Only as you begin to perceive the nature of *I* in its oneness with God do you begin to perceive the nature of your true identity and of the Christhood which is your true identity, which is come that you might have life and that you might have it more abundantly: eternally, infinitely, with enough to give twelve basketsful away to others every day of the week and still have more than enough.

The whole secret of the Master is in the word *I.* Only when you begin to perceive that I and the Father are one can you look in the mirror and say, "Oh, that is not I: that is my body. I am the temple of God. I am in my Father, and my Father is in me. I am in the Christ, and the Christ is in me. I am one with the Father, one, as the branch of the tree is one with the tree."

You are the temple of the living God. Your consciousness is the temple of the living God, and the presence of God is there that you might have life and that you might have it more abundantly.

> *I* am your bread and your meat.
> *I* am your resurrection. *I* am life eternal because
> "I and my Father are one," and not two.
> "I and my Father are one," and I am in Him,
> and He is in me, for we are one.
> And in that oneness I have my allness.

Recognizing the One Selfhood

It would seem as if the world were filled with innumerable persons, separate, one from another, each with a life separate from the other, each with an interest separate from the other. When you begin to perceive the spiritual truth of oneness, you will know that we are all one. There is only one life, one and the same life in everyone, one and the same soul, one and the same spirit, one and the same being.

For this reason the Master gave a long sermon on this principle: "Inasmuch as ye have done it unto one of the least of these my brethren, ye have done it unto me. . . . Inasmuch as ye did it not to one of the least of these ye did it not to me." [21] Why? Because I and the least of these are one, not two separate ones. Every time you injure one of the least of these, you injure yourself, and every time you are a blessing to anyone on the face of the globe, you are a blessing unto yourself. I am the selfhood of you, and you are the selfhood of me, and unless we treat each other with that sacredness, respect, dignity, and love, we are not loving our neighbor as ourself, and our neighbor is our self.

It Is Up to You

Feed this truth of the one Self into your mind morning, noon, and night, and see what happens to you in your relationship with other people and their relationship with you. Feed this into your mind. How did the Master say it? "If ye abide in me, and my words abide in you,"[22] you will bear fruit richly. The responsibility is on your shoulders. Abide in the word or abide not in the word. It is up to you.

In one way it is not up to you. Until you are ready for it, you cannot embrace it. It is not any different with the spiritual life than it is with the artistic life. If you do not understand paintings, you cannot enjoy them and you will not spend your money for them. If you do not know music, you will not enjoy it. There has to be a response within you that makes the spiritual life live, or there is nothing you can do about it. You cannot force yourself to live in the word of God and keep the word of God living in you. You really have to love it with all your heart, with all your soul, with all your mind, or you will love the rest of the things of this world so much that they will occupy your time.

You have only to look around you at your friends and notice those who have made their life a dedication to truth. Notice the degree in which they have abided in the word and have let the word abide in them, and watch the fruitage of their lives: the peace, the safety, the security, the harmony. It is not always true of their relatives. No matter how high you may go in consciousness, you cannot take all your relatives with you because each one is individual in that each person must come to the Father by himself. No one can drag you in. You cannot join any organization that will take you there. You cannot even join a little group of your own and take those who become a part of that group there.

Each must reach the throne of God under his own steam, and it all depends on what degree that love of God has been planted in an individual. And if it is not there, he will have to tarry awhile until it comes. If it does not come in this incarnation, at least you have the satisfaction of knowing that you will live again and again and again, until in the end every knee will bend to God. Just as you have lived many times before and may not have come to the place of loving the Lord your God with all your soul, and you may attain it in this life, so there will be many who will not attain it on this plane but who will attain it the next time around. At least you are always offering a cup of cold water. You are offering it to those who seek it and further than this you cannot go.

Does this clarify for you the reason meditation plays such a great part in the message of the Infinite Way? Can you see that it is in the moments of silence and stillness that the Father reveals these truths to you, and the Word is heard? You do not have to meditate for long periods, although eventually you do learn to be still and silent for five minutes, ten, or fifteen. Some people develop to the place where they can meditate for hours, but very few. For the most part, meditation is a matter of minutes, and just a few minutes. But that is enough to open you, to make you receptive and responsive to the still small voice within. Be assured when It does speak, you have had your God-experience, and from there on you tabernacle with God. Then it becomes natural to go within and commune with God.

TAPE RECORDED EXCERPTS
Prepared by the Editor

Over and over again we are reminded that the goal of the Infinite Way is not to change bad humanhood into good humanhood or to glorify human goodness, but to rise above both the good and the bad. Does not this of necessity involve a dying to the personal sense of life, a relinquishment of our desires, hopes, and fears? As human beings, we cling to these desires, hopes, and fears. Because of that, we go through an inner struggle, which may find outer expression in the loss of all we hold dear or in other serious problems until there is a crossing out or crucifixion of all earthly bonds. Out of this "crossing out" or crucifixion of personal sense comes the rebirth or resurrection.

The nature of this crucifixion is brought out clearly in the following excerpts:

Crucifixion

"Many people turn to truth purely for the purpose of finding a way to overcome their human problems, and they measure their spiritual progress by how many problems they do not have. This is a false measuring rod. There undoubtedly comes a time when the complete absence of problems means spiritual demonstration. Jesus attained that *after* the crucifixion, after the resurrection; but I am afraid too many of us are trying to attain it before the crucifixion. . . and it isn't going to be done. Let it be clearly understood that we will have to make our demonstration over the beliefs of what we call the human mind, before we attain complete liberation."

Joel S. Goldsmith, "Lesson on Grace,"
The 1958 London Closed Class.

"The principle of Good Friday is the principle of the crucifixion of personal selfhood, personal sense, a crucifixion of the belief that we of ourselves have qualities of good or quantities of good. And then comes the resurrection in the realization, 'I am nothing, but *I* can give you all.' Why? 'The Father within me, he doeth the works.' This is the principle of self-renunciation, the principle of crucifixion, the principle of self-abnegation, in which, when we have brought to light the nothingness of our human selfhood, we then reveal the allness, immortality, and eternality of our being.

"We were born the man of earth, and that is what we remain until the crucifixion. That is what we remain as long as we are in the business of glorifying self, building up self. Paul tells us of our other self, that man who has his being in Christ, that is, spiritual man or the divine self. That is the man we are when we can say, 'I can do all things through Christ,' through the spirit of God in me, through the presence of the Father within me. This is no more the man of earth. This is no more the man who says, 'I am wise; I am smart; I am holy; I am spiritual.' No, that man has been thoroughly crucified, and now we have a man who says, 'By the grace of God, I can share with you. By the grace of God, I am guided wisely in my affairs. By the grace of God, I can give and, by the grace of God, I can receive. By the grace of God, I can do: I can do all things through Christ.'"

Joel S. Goldsmith, "Maundy Thursday, Good Friday, Easter: Esoteric Meaning," *The 1959 Maui Advanced Work.*

"The real, the spiritual crucifixion is when you, yourself, crucify yourself in attempting to give up all miracle works. You see how you crucify yourself when someone asks you for help and you have to train yourself not to give it: not to try to reduce the fever, not to try to reduce the lump, not to try to overcome deafness and blindness. You will see how you are crucifying your self, your personal sense, your do-gooding sense. . . . When you experience God, miracles take place out in the world, but don't get hypnotized by miracles. . . . Every time that you can restrain yourself from trying to improve human conditions, you are crucifying your own personal sense, and you are rising into the higher state of spiritual sonship."

Joel S. Goldsmith, "Material or Mental Sense of
Demonstration, Spiritual Unfoldment or Grace,"
The 1963 Instructions for Teaching the Infinite Way.

"You must 'die daily': you must die to matter; you must die
to mortality in order that you may be reborn of the Spirit. But
none of this dying is a process that happens to us: it is a process
that we make happen by our conscious determination: I consciously die daily to the belief that I of my own self am something. I consciously die daily to the belief that there are powers
outside of me influencing my life. . . . On the other hand, I am
consciously reborn every minute of every day in which I can
realize that the spirit of God dwelleth in me, the spirit of God
is upon me, and I am ordained."

Joel S. Goldsmith, "My Consciousness of Truth Makes It
the Law unto Me," *The 1961 Hawaiian Village Open Class.*

Chapter Five

The Function of the
Christ in Us

Some students may wonder what it is that makes the message of the Infinite Way difficult. The way is not easy, but it becomes easier if we know where the difficulty lies. To begin with, the message of the Infinite Way is not a message that can be understood solely with the mind. Even if the message were understood through the mind, that would not make it demonstrable in our experience. Going beyond knowing the truth, therefore, becomes the most important work of this message.

There are certain things that we can learn with the mind and then act out from that knowledge. We can learn how to drive an automobile, how to pilot an airplane, how to build a bridge or a house. We can learn all these things with the mind, and then go out and do them, but no person can learn to paint a great picture, play the piano or sing and make music, unless there is a quality in him that goes beyond the mind. True, anybody can take a brush and make something that looks like a man or a woman, and probably anybody can play the piano and make a tune come out of it, but this is not music, and the other is not art. To bring forth music or art, something more than an understanding of the principles of painting or music is necessary, and that something more is called soul. Without a soul, a painter is not an artist, nor a musician a musician.

With the Mind,
God Cannot Be Proved

So it is that when we are studying a message that has God as its basis, we have to go beyond the mind: we have to reach the soul. A very prominent scientist has written, and it is often quoted, that the existence of God cannot be mathematically proved. I am not enough of a mathematician to know whether or not that is correct, but I am willing to take his word that God cannot be mathematically or scientifically proved. To prove God, we have to go beyond what we see, hear, taste, touch, or smell.

Let me illustrate this. There are those who say, "Look at the beautiful flowers, feel the zephyr-like breeze, and look at the beautiful moon, the stars, and the sun." They say that these prove God. Yes, and then along comes a hurricane. The question now has to come up: where is God? Surely, God is not in that wind, not in that storm, not in the destruction of the flowers or the trees. And our mathematical friends could well say, "Now, where is your God?"

I have traveled the ocean, and I have written that I find God between the waves and the sky. Out on the ocean, I find God very close at hand. Then along comes a great big storm that takes a ship and turns it upside down, and hundreds of people are lost. Somebody says, "Where is your God?"

We cannot prove God by looking at nature, because for every form of good in nature there is a destructive form in nature. Some persons look at the beautiful birds and the beautiful animals and try to prove God. Then when we go out into their domain and see how one eats the other, how cruel one is to another, we cannot but wonder where God is in those birds and animals.

If we could prove God, we must go beyond what we can see,

what we can hear, taste, touch, or what we can smell. We must go beyond the mind, because for every bit of God that we can prove with our mind, somebody will show us the other side and say, "Now, where is your God?"

God-Realized Is the Answer

A spiritual message gives us the answer, because when we bring our God-awareness to the storm, the storm stops. The storm cannot continue if there is a realized presence of God there. A storm is destructive only because there is an absence of God-awareness. It makes no difference how many human beings there may be offering up their prayers. None of that is the proof of the presence of God, because nobody can bring God to the scene by praying in the accepted sense of prayer. If human beings could do that, there would be no storms at sea, because when there is a storm immediately almost everybody begins to pray. But when the presence of God is brought to a storm, the storm stops, no matter how deadly it may appear to be. When the presence of God is brought to animals that prey upon one another, they stop it. They are preying upon one another only because there is an absence of God. There may be many religious human beings around, but there is not God, Itself, realized.

If we were to take the literal statement that God is omnipresent, then God must fill all space, and nowhere on earth could there be a sin, a disease, or a death. In the presence of God, there can be no discordant conditions. If there were, then God would not be omnipotent; God would not be too pure to behold iniquity; God would not be omniscient, all-knowledge. When we take the statement that God is omnipresent, literally, that is entirely correct, for God is omnipresence.

There were some persons in Europe in the last half century, however, who would scarcely have agreed that omnipresence was omnipresent all the time and in all places. Many things took place in Europe during World War II that did not testify to the presence of God and would certainly give atheists the opportunity of saying, "See, there could have been no God there, or this could not have happened." They would be right: there was no God there. God is omnipresent, but God is nowhere until God is realized. Until somebody somewhere actually has the realization of the presence of God, there is no God in operation. That is why these horrors could take place. They could not have taken place in the presence of Jesus Christ; they could not have taken place in the presence of Moses; they could not have taken place in the presence of Elijah. Where those men were, the presence of God was.

Consider the world, its many sicknesses and the great suffering of many thousands today. Notice the much praying to God, even the trips to Lourdes, and how, under ordinary circumstances, if some doctor does not come along with a discovery or some appropriate procedure to cure these persons, they die. God does not save them. If some medicine or surgery is not discovered or administered, they die.

Then notice the difference when those who are on the spiritual path are confronted with the same conditions and call for spiritual help. The spiritually endowed practitioner brings to a situation the actual presence of God, and where the presence of God is, there is liberty and there is healing. Wherever Jesus walked, there was healing, there was forgiveness of sin, and there was supplying. Wherever any spiritually minded practitioner exists, there must be healing. It does not mean that everyone gets healed, because frankly everyone is not receptive to spiritual healing.

A Desire to Know God Makes for a Receptivity to Spiritual Healing

To be receptive to spiritual healing means that there must be an innate desire for God, not just a great desire to be healed.

There is no virtue in that. Everybody in the world wants to be well, so that he can work and take care of his family. The fertile ground for spiritual healing is in the individual who wants not merely to be healed—being healed is a natural desire—but who along with this says, "Of course, I want to be healed, but that is not my major problem. Above all things, I want to know God. Above all things, I must know God. I do not want to pass from this earth before I have come face to face with God. I want to know the secret behind this universe. I want to know the cause of life."

There are relatively few who turn to spiritual healing, and how very few there are who have that deep intense desire to know God. Most of us, when we came to a metaphysical or spiritual teaching, came for healing. That is perfectly legitimate, because it is one of the ways that nature has of driving us back to God. But even though we receive our healing, and many do receive healing even before that desire for God is awakened, that desire is awakened by the intensity of the spiritual power flowing through the practitioner or teacher. Sometimes practitioners and teachers are so deeply imbued with the spirit of God that most of those who come to them are raised up in some degree, whether or not they want anything more than the healing.

God Is Not a Messenger Boy

We can always search ourselves when we are on this path to see to what extent the desire for God is the desire that something will be accomplished. Let me explain why this is a barrier and why this often prevents the very thing we are hoping to achieve. Let us say I have a desire to be healed, to be made happy, to be made prosperous. So I am going to go to God. Watch this! I am going to God, but am I going to God for God? No, I am going to God to get what I am looking for, so God is going to be my messenger boy. He is going to go and get what I want for me. Do you see how that proves to be a barrier?

God is not a messenger boy. God is the health of our countenance, and when we have God, we have health. What mistakes we make! Me, God, health! Me, God, supply! Me, God, companionship! "Dear God, go out, please, get it for me." God becomes our servant. There is no such God to begin with, so it is all in the realm of imagination. For centuries orthodox religion has taught that there is a God who is our servant. Just tell God what we want, and Santa Claus will deliver it to our doorstep on December 25, or sooner. There is no such God, and we create a barrier in our consciousness the moment we go to God with our vision on something other than God.

God is our supply. God does not get supply; God does not give supply; God does not send supply; God *is* supply. God does not supply us with companions: God is the only companion. When we have the companionship of God, we have the companionship of each other, because our union with God unites us with one another. Our union with God unites us with our supply; our union with God unites us with our health. Therefore, the moment we think of God *and* something, we have lost our demonstration.

All we have to do is go back in our memory and think how we have offended. We have not offended God; we have just offended against ourselves, against our demonstration, because there is no God that can do something. There is only a God that can *be* something, and what God is, is life. So God cannot *send* us life eternal; God cannot *give* us life eternal: God *is* our eternal life. God cannot give us our daily bread: God *is* our daily bread, and when we have God, we not only have our daily bread, we have twelve basketsful left over.

Seek God Only for God

Many of us, until we awaken to this truth, stand in the way of our own healing, of our supply, and even in the way of our demonstration of happiness, because we are seeking God for a purpose. In other words, we are seeking God only as a way-station. We are going to stop off at God in order to reach what we are looking for.

If we have wandered from the spiritual path by seeking God for a reason, we have set up the barrier to our demonstration in our own consciousness. Therefore, we must go back, begin all over again, and realize, "Seek ye first the kingdom of God, and his righteousness; and all these things shall be added unto you."[1] We must seek only the kingdom of God, seek only the realization of God, seek only the inner contemplation of God. This is not as difficult as it sounds, because it is not far-off from any one of us. The kingdom of God is within, and every truly holy man or holy book will turn us back within ourselves and show us that unless we find the kingdom of God within ourselves, we cannot find it in our human affairs. But if we do find the kingdom of God within ourselves, we find the activity of God in all our affairs.

A God of Spirit Cannot Be Known With the Mind

This is why we must go beyond the mind and what it thinks. A Russian flier came back from space and said, "I found no God up in space, so there is no God." He could look up in space, down beneath the earth, or up above the sky, and he would never find God, because God cannot be seen with human eyesight. "God is a spirit: and they that worship him must worship him in spirit and in truth"[2]—not as something tangible to the sight, not as something that we see, hear, taste, touch, or smell, not something that is out doing favors for us.

God must be recognized as spirit. What is spirit? Ah, that is why we say, "God is spirit," because nobody knows what spirit is. If we knew what spirit is, we would know what God is, and that is impossible. It is not possible to know God with the mind: it is possible to know God only through the spirit, and when we study a spiritual message, we are developing that spiritual center in us that knows God.

The human being can never know God. Only when the spirit of God dwells in him, only when this spiritual center is opened and developed, only then is it possible to know God, because spirit only knows spirit.

Was it not made clear, "We know not what we should pray for as we ought"[3]—or what things to pray for? But there is a spirit in each one of us which is the connecting link with God. When we develop that connecting link, we never have to speak to God, we never have to ask anything of God; we never have to tell anything to God; we never have to try to influence God. From then on, our contact with God is a communion, an inner feeling:

"I and my Father are one."[4]
The Father within me bears witness with my spirit.
"The spirit of the Lord God is upon me."[5]
His spirit dwells in me.
"I live; yet not I, but Christ liveth in me."[6]
This spiritual center lives in me.

Of course it does not make sense to the mathematician, who is immersed in theory; of course it does not make sense to anybody who is trying to understand God with the mind, or anybody who is trying through human prayer to get God to do something. God does not respond to human urging and God certainly can never be controlled or influenced by man. It is the other way around: God must influence man; God must control man; God must speak to man—not man to God: God to man.

Inviting God to Reveal Itself Is Prayer

When we have reversed ourselves so that we do not pray to God in the sense of imparting any of our desires or wishes to

God, when we are through with that nonsense, our prayer
becomes a uniting and communing with God:

> "I and my Father are one." Thy spirit is "closer. . .
> than breathing, and nearer than hands and feet."[7]
> Where Thou art, I am. Where Thou art is holy
> ground. Thy spirit pervades and animates me.
> Thy spirit within me is the very life of me.
> "Thine is the kingdom, and the glory and the
> power"[8]—Thine! And all this is within me.
> "The Father that dwelleth in me, he doeth the
> works."[9] Greater is He that is within me than
> any he out here, than any problem that is without.

As we live with these truths, as we make these truths our
own, live with them morning, noon, and night, pray without
ceasing, pray that we may feel the presence of God with us, in
the attitude of "Speak, Lord; for thy servant heareth,"[10] always
inviting God to speak to us, always inviting God to impart
Himself to us, always inviting God to share with us, this is
prayer. This is spiritual prayer; this is mystical prayer. This is the
prayer that avails much, because it is not seeking for worldly
things. Instead it is a desire to return to the Father's house.
Recognizing ourselves as the prodigal, our prayer is:

> Father, let me come back to Thy house
> to be one with Thee. I have wandered out here
> in the world too long, witnessing that separate
> and apart from Thee there is nothing but trouble,
> separate and apart from Thee
> there is nothing but woe.

> Let me go back within me, let us unite within me:
> "I and my Father are one." Let me feel this oneness;
> let me know this oneness.

> Let me abide in Thee, and Thou in me—
> not because I want You to do
> something for me,
> but just because
> I want my original relationship,
> the relationship that I had with You in the beginning,
> before the world was, the relationship of oneness.

Oneness! This was the original relationship between God and man. Oneness! "Son, thou art ever with me, and all that I have is thine."[11] We are one, not two; not You up there and me here, but the two of us are right here: God the Father, and God the Son, both here. This must be realized. It does not make any difference what we may own or how many possessions we have. If we do not know this truth, it is of no avail to us. It is the *knowing* that makes all good available to us. The truth will not help us: it is the *knowing* of the truth: "Ye shall know the truth,"[12] and we must *know* that our basic relationship with the Father is oneness.

The Fruitage of Conscious Contact

As we live with these truths within ourselves, we are developing a soul-center. It is already there, tightly closed, because of centuries of non-use. Every one of us has the indwelling Christ. Everyone, at every level of life, has Christ incarnate in him. Paul said it: "Christ liveth in me." The Christ lives in every individual in this world.

As Saul of Tarsus, Paul had reached a place where, because of the intense drive within him to know God, even though he was doing it in a wrong manner, he succeeded, and when he had the experience of the Christ, from then on, the Christ dwelt in him, and the Christ became his life. So with us.

Throughout our human experience, up to a certain point even though the kingdom of God is within us, even though the

Christ is incarnate in us, it is of no use to us. It is only when we become aware of It, when the Christ announces Itself to us, when we feel that indwelling presence, when something within us says, "Ah, this is it! I have made contact! 'I and my Father are one!'" then the spirit of God lives our life, and we have the experience that baffles all materialists.

We have a greater sense of youth, a greater sense of vitality, a greater sense of strength, a greater sense of health, a greater sense of supply. We experience less fear, less woe, less trouble, and the materialists cannot see what is doing it. They ask, because they are surprised, and they are sure that we have a hidden secret. But we cannot reveal the "pearl."[13] to them. In the first place, they would not recognize it; in the second place, they would trample on it, because it is so indefinable that it cannot be known except in one way, and that is by an inner feeling and an inner awareness of it.

It is as if there were two, this something within which is always bubbling, this something within which brings the smile to the face for no outer reason. That is why very often our joy is questioned. "How can you be so joyous in this world?" It is because we are not reacting to this world, because there is something inside that sees behind the scene, and sees how mankind could be free of all these problems. It will not be, not for a long time to come, because it does not want to follow this way.

Not Victories, but Glories

Mankind wants to be free in its own way; it wants to attain freedom through victory over someone or something. That is mankind's greatest weakness, the desire for victory. Victory always means that somebody loses, and somebody losing always means somebody else seeking to be a victor again. It is always back and forth, and back and forth. In one battle one person is on top, and in the next battle someone else is on top, but it is always a battle because there is always someone who wants a victory.

Victory is not the way. There is a spirit in man that brings about his freedom without victories, without warfare, without battles. The Bible is full of statements showing that once we have contacted the spirit within us, we no longer need to resort to the weapons of this world. There is a higher force operating, which the world cannot understand, which brings us our glories, not our victories, our glories: our health, supply, friendship, happiness. These are not victories: these are glories, because to get them we did not have to take them from somebody else. We did not have to make somebody else lose in order that we might win.

Supply May Come Through, Not From, a Person

In the earlier years of my work, when the thought present-ed itself that since my supply was coming from people, every time my supply came in, somebody had less of supply, the nature of my prayer changed. It went something along this line, not exactly, but this is the essence of it: Father, I do not want what is already out here. That belongs to somebody else. Let my supply come from within. Let it come from new channels; let it come in new ways, so that if anyone shares with me, he is only a transfer agent, and that transfer does not lessen his supply. If anything, let it increase his supply. Let me not believe that it comes from those who share, so that they have less. If it must come through someone, let it come *through* him, not *from* him. Then, in the giving, they have nothing less, but rather more.

My prayer all my life since then has always been: Father, let it be so. Let the loaves and fishes be multiplied by the spirit within me. This leaves me with much glory, but with no victo-ries and no depriving anyone, no taking from anyone what he may have need of. It is the glory of being abundantly supplied and having the consciousness that no one is being deprived of anything because of it.

The Christ: the Multiplier, the Healer, the Forgiver

The whole secret is that there is the Christ, the spirit, or son of God within us, and It is a multiplier. It multiplied loaves and fishes of old; It multiplies our loaves and fishes now. In fact, the function of the Christ that dwells within us is to heal the sick, raise the dead, forgive the sinner, multiply loaves and fishes. It was there before Abraham was; It will be there unto the end of the world.

> "I will never leave thee, nor forsake thee,"[14]
> *I* will be with thee to the end of the world,
> *I*, this Christ, that is innate in every one of us.

We have never been separated from this Christ; we have separated ourselves in belief by ignoring It, or in many cases, believing It was something that lived two thousand years ago in the Holy Land. It did, but It never left. It was never crucified; It never went to heaven, not the Christ. The Christ is the indwelling spirit of God that is incarnate in every individual. It constitutes our oneness with God; It constitutes our relationship with God, because It is the son of God in us.

Instead of looking out here in the world to persons, the more we ponder and think about the indwelling Christ, this spirit of the Father within us that does the works, this spirit that multiplies the loaves and fishes, the deeper becomes our realization of our relationship to It.

The function of this indwelling spirit is to heal the sick, raise the dead, forgive the sinners, and multiply loaves and fishes. We are perfectly willing for the Christ to heal and feed us. Are we as willing that the Christ forgive the sinner? Yes, if we are the sinner! How completely have we surrendered the desire for revenge, for satisfaction, for someone's punishment? How completely have we accepted the doctrine of forgiving seventy times seven? How completely have we been able to say within ourselves, "I hold no man in bondage to any sin of the past, present, or future, and I am in agreement that the Christ within me should forgive, and forgive seventy times seven"?

The Christ Is in Man to Bless All Mankind

We do not release ourselves to the Christ unless we are willing for the Christ to have full action in us, not just the action of feeding us, not just the action of healing us. It must have the free action of forgiving, and not only forgiving us. Nor must we think of the Christ as feeding and healing us above all others. Perhaps there is the great barrier. We think that the Christ, if we have It, has been given to us to feed us, to heal us, to forgive us. That is the least part of the function of the Christ. Once we have recognized that Christ, we will not need any more forgiving, we will not need any more feeding, we will not need any more healing.

What was the function of the Christ in Jesus? Was it to heal Jesus? Was it to feed Jesus? Was it to forgive Jesus? Is the function of the Christ any different in us? We must give up this belief that God planted the Christ in us just for our special benefit. The function of the Christ in man is to bless mankind, to raise up those who are still in sin, those who are still in disease, those who are still in death, those who are still in lack. This is the function of the Christ in us and in every person who is awakened to Its present.

That is why, in every spiritual teaching in the world, it has been said that the secret of supply is not in getting: it is in giving. Some persons understand that, and they know full well that the amount of supply they get is not supply; it is the amount of supply they can pour out that is really supply. But let us go a step further now. Let us realize that the function of the Christ in man is to bless, to heal, to raise, to redeem, to forgive, to feed, to companion with one another and the world.

As we contemplate the Christ in us, let us remember that the Christ that lives our life has not been given to us for our picayune little satisfaction, health, or life. The Christ has been given to us that we may be transparencies for God, that we may show forth God's glory on earth. That is why the Christ is in us: to show forth God's glory in healing, in forgiving, in redeeming, in supplying. We open ourselves to the Christ-activity by inviting the world, not outwardly through advertising, but spiritually within, inviting the world to our spiritual household, inviting this world to come and eat and drink, letting this world come and be healed through the inner realization:

> Thank You, Father, I know why the Christ is here in
> me. I am willing for It to function. I am willing to be
> the instrument to heal, to feed, to forgive, and to
> redeem all whom Thou sendest me.

Then we have opened ourselves, and we will find that as the Christ functions for the benefit of others, we are included. We do not have to be specifically wanting Its action for ourselves: we are just included in Its action without taking thought.

Awakening to the Christ Within

God has not planted His spirit in us for our glory. He has planted His spirit in us for His glory, to show forth God's glory on earth as it is in heaven. "The heavens declare the glory of God; and the firmament sheweth his handiwork,"[15] and the Christ in us is for the purpose of showing forth God's grace to man.

The least we can do is to let the Christ that is within us forgive those who may have offended us, those who may have offended our race, our religion, our nation, those who in any way may have offended against us. Let this Christ forgive them, for the Christ does not judge or condemn, but forgives. Let this Christ that is within us feed the hungry, heal the sick, and raise the dead. We are not called upon to do it with our understanding. Our understanding will never be great enough to heal a headache.

There is not a person I have ever met on this earth who knows enough about healing to heal, not even those who have written twenty books about it. It is the spirit that does the healing work. All this truth-knowing does is to help to lift us up to where the spirit that is in us can function. That is the purpose of all Infinite Way books, to help open this spiritual center, to help put us in an atmosphere of the spirit so that the spirit can function.

Jesus knew that he could not heal. Did he not say, "I can of mine own self do nothing"[16]? It is the Father within us; it is the spirit within that does the work. But something or other has to bring this spirit to life. That we do through our study and meditation. The more we dwell in the word that the kingdom of God is within us and realize its nature and its function, the more we are awakening to this Christ within us, which has been dormant insofar as our experience is concerned.

When we have overcome that unfortunate habit of going to God for something, we are then able to get quiet inside and be in a listening state of receptivity. Eventually we hear the still, small voice:

> *I* am with you. *I* have never left you.
> *I* will be with you unto the end of the world.
> Fear not, *I* am with you.
> My peace, give *I* unto you.

That is the secret. There is this transcendental presence we call the Christ that is within us, and It gives us a peace, the kind of peace the world cannot give. It is an entirely different kind of peace, and yet it results out here in human harmony. It results in health, supply, and companionship, but it does not know anything about those things. It gives us the inner peace which translates itself out here in human terms as forms of good.

The moment we hear, *"My* peace I give; *My* kingdom is established within you; *My* grace is upon thee," and we have that awareness of an inner something other than ourselves, we have attained our conscious union with our source, and from then on, this that says

> *"My"* is always with us.
> *My* peace do I give. *My* grace is thine.
> Fear not, *I* am with thee.

Then we understand why it is not possible for the person with only a mental comprehension of truth to make his demonstration, because the demonstration actually is made from within by this presence, this spirit of God in man, this that we call the indwelling Christ.

Scripture tells us that God is not in the whirlwind: God is in the "still small voice." [17] The moment that still small voice speaks in us, the earth melts, whether it is a storm, a sin, a disease, whatever it may be. None of that is possible to the person who is operating entirely on the mental level. He may know it all in his mind, but until there is an answering response from within, he has not yet made contact with the son of God that dwells in him for the very purpose of establishing harmony on earth as it is in heaven. It is the function of the Christ in the midst of us to establish that harmony on earth. The Christ in us is the connecting link between God's government and this earth.

TAPE RECORDED EXCERPTS
Prepared by the Editor

There is much confusion about the role the mind plays in our experience, so much so that students sometimes attempt to make the mind a total blank. When the mind is put in its proper place, we will no longer try to blank it out, nor will we go to the other extreme of using it in an attempt to create our good or draw it to us.

The mind is an instrument to be used for the activity of awareness, awareness of the infinity and glory of the consciousness that we are, unfolding to us in proportion to our awareness of It. We become aware as we stop using the mind as a power to create our good, and it then becomes a transparency for consciousness, a state of receptivity to spiritual activity.

"Mind as an Instrument"

"Rightly speaking mind is not God, and God is not mind. . . . Mind is our instrument. . . of awareness. Through the mind, we become aware; through the mind we even have the ability to reason out, to think. . . . God neither reasons nor thinks. God is being, and God is being without thinking something out, planning it, or reasoning it out. But that which we call God-consciousness, which is a state of pure being or pure knowing, is impossible to us in our human stage. Therefore, we are given a mind, the activity of which becomes our avenue of awareness, our thinking, reasoning, planning mind. . . .

"It is not the activity of your mind that frees anybody. It is the activity of truth in your mind that frees him. . . . Anyone who has ever practiced and used the mind in his practice will testify to the fact that he is worn out long before the day is over, tired physically and mentally and usually with a pain across the back of the neck at the base of the brain. He has been using the mind to try to create something out here in space, to change something in the body or in the pocketbook. That is not the function of the mind; that is not the function of spiritual wisdom."

Joel S. Goldsmith, "Idolatry,"
The First 1953 New York Closed Class.

Chapter Six

What Have You
in the House?

The kingdom of God is within us, but to experience the good of that kingdom, we must open out a way for the splendor and glory already established within us to escape. The truth is that everything concerning our life is already within us.

In the human world, however, we go outside ourselves for everything. We try to get what we want from other people or circumstances. Everything in human life is focused outside, ignoring totally the fact that every real value is already established within us and that we can have the harmony of life, the health, the prosperity, the success, and the joy if only we will go to the kingdom of God for it, instead of seeking it out in the world.

The way to release this spiritual presence and spiritual power is through meditation. So, as Infinite Way students, our day always begins with meditation. From the time we awaken in the morning, even before getting out of bed, we meditate. We meditate at breakfast time; we meditate on leaving home; we meditate at noon, at night, and when we awaken in the middle of the night.

Scripture reminds us:

> I am the bread of life.
>
> John 6:35

> I am the way, the truth, and the life.
>
> John 14:6

> I am the resurrection, and the life.
>
> John 11:25

> I have meat to eat that ye know not of.
>
> John 4:32

> Whosoever drinketh of the water
> that I shall give him shall never thirst.
>
> John 4:14

Since Jesus had no bucket with which to draw the water, from whence came this water? From the invisible wellspring of water within him.

So it is then that the bread of life, the staff of life, the water, the wine, the resurrection, and the life eternal are within us where that *I* is, for *"I am the bread of life."* This bread, meat, wine, water, this spiritual presence, and spiritual power are all within us. How foolish to look outside for it if the good that we seek in our life is already within us! How many people are there who have found something outside and then later learned that it was not that which gave them their lasting good, their lasting peace, their lasting harmony or success!

Releasing Our Good From Within

If the kingdom of God is within us, we must find a way to let it flow out from us. The Hebrew prophet Elijah asked the poor widow for help. He seemed completely unfeeling about her sad plight, the fact that she was about to lose her son in slavery because of debt, and instead of helping her asked her for "a morsel of bread."[1] When she protested, "As the Lord thy God liveth, I have not a cake, but an handful of meal in a barrel, and a little oil in a cruse: and, behold, I am gathering two sticks, that I may go in and dress it for me and my son, that we may eat it, and die."[2] Elijah still insisted that she make him a cake, which she did with the result that "the barrel of meal wasted not, neither did the cruse of oil fail."[3]

Even in this modern day a spiritual teacher would be thought to be very cruel if some poor widow asked for help and her teacher were to say, "What have you in the house?" But this is a spiritual principle. Elijah had no way of helping her except spiritually. He had no money, and yet the spiritual help had to become tangible in her human experience as supply. The prophet realized that the question was not what he could give her, not what he could go out and get for her, but "What have you?" So when the widow discovered that she had a few drops of oil and a little meal, which she must have looked upon as a mere nothing, Elijah pointed up the principle of supply by asking her to bake him a cake, in other words, to take that meal and oil and do something with it, which she did. The cruse of oil never ran dry; her supply began when she began to pour, when she began to give from what she already had.

When the Master was called upon to feed the multitude he also asked, "How many loaves have ye?"[4] He too received a negative answer, "Five, and two fishes."[5] What use would they be among so many? Again the Master used this spiritual principle of supply and "blessed, and brake the loaves."[5] When they began using what they already had, it began to multiply until there was enough for everybody and twelve basketsful left over.

So it is when we are confronted with any kind of a problem. The first thought is how are we going to solve it, and usually we immediately think of something out here. But our first thought should be, "What have I in the house?" Then we can turn within ourselves:

Father, what have I in the house?
What is there in my consciousness
that would meet this need?
What is there in my consciousness
that would fulfill this purpose?
What have I in my consciousness that I can pour,
that I can break, that I can share,
that I can give?
What is there in me that will solve this problem?

Such a contemplation reveals why meditation is the way of the spiritual life. In quiet meditation we close our eyes, although some people find it just as convenient to keep them open, but closing our eyes is symbolic of shutting out the world, so that we can contemplate within ourselves:

Father, here is a problem and,
since the kingdom of God is within me,
that means the solution is within me.
The substance, the supply, the law,
the truth, or whatever it is
that will meet this need is already within me.
Now what is it?
How can I begin to pour?
How can I begin to share?

In such a meditation it is not very long before some kind of an answer comes forth. It may not come forth in words, and yet it may. It may come forth just as an awareness, as if there were a release: "Ah! it's solved. I am sure God is on the field." Sometimes a very specific instruction comes. Sometimes the words will come, "Forgive more," or "Pray for your enemies."

A Spiritual Master Turns Within
for the Necessary Solution

In one way or another this practice of turning within leads us to seek the answer instead of running up and down the world looking for the solution. Rather than expecting it to come from people in the world, we learn to go within ourselves. Where could Moses go when he stood with the Red Sea in front of him and Pharaoh's army in back of him? To whom was he going to go and where was he going to go for help except within himself?

Where is Jesus going to go for spiritual wisdom with a multitude to feed, a multitude to heal, or a multitude to teach? To whom is he going to go? If his disciples had had enough to meet the need, he would not have been the teacher. There was nowhere to go and no one to whom to go. He had to go to the Father within himself; he had to go to the divine principle of life; he had to go to the source of life and truth and learn to let it flow out.

There is a passage of scripture that says: "And this is life eternal, that they might know thee the only true God."[6] It is safe to assume that we do not know God and, as a matter of fact, that very few people in the history of the world have ever known God. Yet to know Him aright is life eternal.

God Can Be Revealed
Only From Within

Perhaps the very first thing we have to learn, therefore, is: What is God? The strange thing is that although we have forty or fifty centuries of religious life behind us, there is not a book to be found anywhere that can tell us what God is. No such book has ever been written. Those who came face to face with God and who knew God were never able to put their revelation or discovery into words and, therefore, we could search the libraries from New York to Rome and we would not find a sin-

gle book that can help us learn what God is. That is a disturb-
ing position in which to be placed. We have to know God
aright, but there are no books to go to, and I might add this:
there are some teachers who know it, but they will not tell. At
least, I have never yet met a teacher who knew who would tell.

So we are face to face with the fact that, if we are to know
God, we are going to have to get that knowledge from within our own consciousness. The secret is there; the secret of
God is within us. It is within every individual, but it is not to
be found easily or lightly. We cannot just turn within and say,
"God, who are You?" or, "God, what are You?" and expect
that the full revelation will come by merely saying those
words. It requires devotion, sincerity, really an earnest desire
to know God aright. There has to be that eagerness, that pas-
sion almost, to know God before God will give up the secret.
Until then, it is hidden within us, within, where eternal life is
to be found.

Importance of Meditation

We all want eternal life, and we all would like to have
health, harmony, and strength throughout our span of human
life, but unfortunately there is no place to get that except within oneself. Therefore, the person who is really hungering and
thirsting after harmonious living right here on earth, the person
who really wants to experience health and strength, who wants
to have possession of his faculties even into his later years has to
make up his mind that he is going to find it.

Meditation is the only way in which one can go within and
eventually find at least some measure of that secret. We want
success in life, whether it is physical success in the form of a
healthy body, professional success, or success in our human relationships: in our marriage and in our family life. Once we realize that that success can come only from within our own being,
we are forced into frequent meditation.

Meditation Releases the Presence Within

It is not that we do not go through all the motions of conducting our business or profession in the same way as we have always done. It only means that, by going within and releasing the presence of God that is pent up within us, we have the presence and power of God animating all that we do, working with us and walking with us. Scripture says it this way: "My presence shall go with thee, and I will give thee rest."[7] *My* presence is behind you and walks beside you.

In the ordinary human life, that is not true. The average human being does not have the spiritual presence going before him, making "the crooked places straight."[8] That is why he so often wanders into crooked places. The human being does not have some presence going before him on the road, keeping his automobile and everyone else's automobile in its rightful place at the right time. Few people have the awareness of a divine presence going before them, beside them, and behind them, and there is a reason for it. That presence is locked up within them, and until they release It, It is not functioning for them.

Meditation releases that presence, and here is the way. The Master said, "Ye shall know the truth, and the truth shall make you free."[9] The whole secret lies in knowing the truth. That means that as we are about to leave home in the morning, whether for business, a profession, or just marketing or shopping, we have to pause for a moment to know the truth that the spirit of God never leaves us or forsakes us. During the day we have business matters to take care of and we are told in scripture that we are not to lean unto our own understanding:[10] His understanding is infinite.

How blessed is a household if the husband or the wife remembers consciously that man's wisdom is not sufficient to run a business, a law office, or a bank, but that the wisdom of God is infinite and omnipresent. "The place whereon thou standest is holy ground,"[11] because the intelligence of God is present where I am, where you are, and where everyone is. Now the breadwinner of the house goes out, not in the limitations of his own wisdom, but clothed with divine wisdom, all because somebody knew the truth, somebody paused for a moment of meditation and realized that the wisdom of God governs him and his affairs, the wisdom of God is the activity of his business, profession, or whatever it may be.

Bringing the Divine Government Into Daily Experience

As far as the world is concerned, the passage of scripture that says, "He performeth the thing that is appointed for me,"[12] is not true. God is not performing all that the people of this world have to do or it would be done better than it is. There would be more intelligence in government, in labor relationships, and in international affairs, if God were performing the work instead of its being performed by stupid, limited man.

But then there it is: "Ye shall know the truth, and the truth shall make you free." The God that performs that which is given us to do does it when, by knowing the truth, we open out a way for that imprisoned God-presence and God-power to do it for us. Regardless of what our task may be at any given moment of the day, it becomes necessary to pause for a second to realize:

The government is on His shoulders.
He performs that which is given me to do,
and He perfects that which concerns me.
His presence goes before me.
I am not alone, for He has promised:
"I will never leave thee, nor forsake thee.[13] . . .
Fear not I am with Thee."[14]

Then when we go about our business, we are not going alone with our own wisdom, our own strength, our own knowledge, or our own power. We have opened out a way, and this imprisoned God-presence and God-power now goes out before us.

Giving Out of Our Conscious Awareness

When the question is asked, "What have you in the house?" is not the answer clear?

I have God; I have God in my house,
in my consciousness; I have God. Wherever I am,
I have God, and that is enough to know.

Anyone who knows that knows what he has in the house, what he can give and what he can share:

I have God. I have God in my consciousness.
I have the kingdom of God within me.
I have the grace of God within me,
and wherever I go I have that to give.

I need never open my mouth. I can keep as silent as
I want to be, and yet I can be a blessing wherever
I am by the recognition that the presence of God is
with me wherever I am, and that presence of
God is a benediction to all whom I meet.

We must be very sure that we want that presence of God to be a benediction to our enemies as well as to our friends. We have to be sure that we want that presence of God to prosper everyone equally. They will not all prosper equally, because they will not all open their consciousness to it, but we have to want it for them; we have to pray for our enemies; we have to forgive seventy times seven. It makes no difference whether they accept it; it makes no difference whether they know it. We are making our demonstration at this moment, and that demonstration calls for what we have in the house, and we have to give it: we have forgiveness and we have love; we have sharing; we have praying for the enemy; we have praying for our friends; we have the kingdom of God within us.

Sharing Material Good

The sharing of our material good is especially important to the persons who have such a fear of the lack of money that they hoard it. For them it is a very good thing to be compelled to break loose and begin giving and sharing, because they may have been making a God out of hoarding their possessions, and as long as they are doing that they cannot expect to make spiritual progress.

The giving of our material goods is really the least of the spiritual graces. If there is somebody who is fearing to give up those last few drops of oil or that last bit of meal, then it is good that in some way or other he be compelled to give. Many years ago a very successful and prosperous practitioner had a patient come one day and ask for help. She told the practitioner that she was not in a position to pay for it, and the practitioner asked why that was the case. She explained that she was a working girl, and it took all that she earned to pay her expenses so that she did not have any money for the practitioner.

His unfeeling response was, "Could you walk to the office instead of riding?"

"Well, yes, it would be possible."

He added, "Could you give up your lunch?"

"Yes, that could be, too."

So he bluntly told her, "Make up your mind either to give up your lunch or part of it and give up your streetcar and at least bring that much into this office."

The girl must have felt that this man was being very cruel and commercial, but she wanted the healing, so she agreed to his terms. Within two weeks she had a healing, a very beautiful healing, and then the practitioner made her a gift of an expensive book and said, "Child, I did not want your money. I wanted to break your fear of money. I wanted to break that sense you had that you could not afford something that is essential to you. You are the very child of God, and there is no limit to what you can have if only you will let loose."

Here again is a case similar to that of the widow, who had to be made to give up her cruse of oil and her meal. There are cases where sometimes a person might be told, "Look into your clothes closet and find some clothing to give away, shoes, or something of that kind to break the mesmerism of believing that money is supply or that money is limited."

Ordinarily when we speak of giving, we do not mean giving in that sense. We mean giving in the sense of what is locked up within us that we probably do not know we have, or what is locked up within us that we have not been in the habit of sharing. When we turn within and ask ourselves, "Have I any substance within me that is decaying for lack of use? Have I any spiritual qualities within myself that I am not bringing forth for the benefit of this world?" we usually find that we have overlooked something.

Praying for the Enemy, a Form of Releasing From Within

At one time a minister, who was not very much in accord with our work and did not see any need for it, said that everything the Christ had was already in his church and, therefore, he could not see why anything further was needed. Then I asked him this question: "In the last war, how many days did you keep your church open to pray for the enemy?"

That shocked him, and he rather testily replied, "Of course, we didn't do anything like that."

"But does not the Bible teach that it profits us nothing to pray for our friends? We must pray for our enemies if we would be children of God and, if children of God, heirs, joint-heirs to all the heavenly riches. Aren't you overlooking an opportunity to get rich and to be fruitful and to multiply?"

Let us not believe for a moment that Christ Jesus was misleading his followers when he said to them, "For if ye love them which love you, what reward have ye?[15]. . . Pray for them which despitefully use you, and persecute you."[16]

There must have been a reason for these commands, and the only way in which we will ever discover whether this is a spiritual law or not is to begin to do that very thing: turn within. We must use that talent that has heretofore been unused, the one of praying for our enemy and watch to see what effect it will have. Another command is that we must lose our life before we can find it.

Living Out From the Kingdom Within

We all have the kingdom of God locked up within us, but we are not sharing it enough. Even we, who are sharing it in a small degree, should not fool ourselves: it is only a tiny bit, just a grain. None of us has really learned how to give fully and completely and, thereby, demonstrate life eternal for himself. We will not demonstrate life eternal; we will not demonstrate health; we will not demonstrate abundant supply until we have learned how to "open out a way for the imprisoned splendor to escape."

Meditation is the way, and the reason is that when a problem arises and we once have accepted the fact that the answer lies within us, that will compel us to meditate. It will compel us, for a moment at least, to close our eyes:

> All right, Father, here is the problem, and the answer
> is within me. What must I do to bring it forth? What
> must I give? What have I to share? What have I in
> my house? What is within me?

Soon the answers begin to come because they are within us, and now we are giving them the opportunity to flow out. A boy of twelve wrote to me that his poorest subject was mathematics and that he was facing an examination which he felt he could not pass. On the day of the examination, he sat for a moment before trying to answer the questions and remembered the passage of scripture his mother had given him for that week: "I can of mine own self do nothing.[17] . . . The Father that dwelleth in me, he doeth the works."[18]

The thought came to him, "Well, even if I can't do this, the Father can," and he not only passed his examination but found that after that, mathematics was easier for him and all his marks went up. Now here was an example of meditation, even though it was but a momentary one, just remembering his Bible passage.

"Man shall not live by bread alone, but by every word that proceedeth out of the mouth of God."[19] The case of the boy taking the examination was a demonstration of the truth that he could not live that day just by his brain-power or his knowledge, but that he lived and passed his examination by virtue of the word of God, by virtue of a scriptural passage of truth entertained in his consciousness.

On the occasion of a class we had in California, one of the students who came left her two children in charge of their grandparents. Then the flu epidemic hit, and the grandparents and the two children went to bed with the flu. The fifteen-year-old girl began to think about this situation and said to herself, "Oh, this cannot go on. We are learning these passages of scripture. We are learning this truth, and it must work. But what truth?"

Then she remembered that one of the passages she had been taught was: "The place whereon thou standest is holy ground," so she thought that if the place whereon she stood was holy ground, everything there must be perfect. Within a few minutes she was out of bed and well. She went to her younger brother with this same truth and then to the grandparents. By suppertime all four of them were at the table. It had taken but a moment of meditation to let something come out from within. It was not medicine that went in. It was spiritual medicine that came out, the word of God.

In a school with quite a large class of ten-year olds, occasionally the teacher of that class would say, "Let us close our eyes for a minute and just meditate." At first the children did not know what it meant to meditate, but it did not take long for them to find out that they were just being still to let God work, and soon they insisted on two meditations every day, one in the morning session and one in the afternoon.

One boy in this class had been almost incorrigible, so disobedient and restless that it seemed that nothing could be done with him or for him. One day the teacher happened to say, "We have to mark these papers, so we will not be able to have our meditation."

At that, the unruly boy jumped up and said, "Please, do not let us miss our meditation." And the very moment that sprang forth from him marked a change in his conduct. It was the beginning of his rebirth.

A Conscious Act

When we begin to perceive that the whole kingdom of God is within us and that we can draw forth everything from it, there is no answer to life except in meditation, in turning within to let the Father within reveal Himself, to let the kingdom of God flow; to let the presence of God go before us to "make the crooked places straight." All this must be done consciously, not by just piously saying, "God is going to take care of everything." It is not that way at all. Releasing the inner kingdom is a conscious act of turning within and making room for infinity to escape, actually seeking specific guidance. Even though it may come in the form of a scriptural passage, it will prove to be humanly practical in the world. The meat the world knows not of and the wellsprings of water are all within us.

When Jesus taught, he was not teaching how great he was, nor was he teaching that he was somebody set apart to do these miraculous things and that when he was gone the world would lose all of it. No, he was teaching principles when he said: "Nevertheless I tell you the truth; It is expedient for you that I go away: for if I go not away, the comforter will not come unto you; but if I depart, I will send him unto you."[20] In other words if we keep relying on some person to make our demonstrations, this comforter, this spirit of God, this truth will not come to us. If we set up any individual or group of individuals as having some divine power which others do not have or which the world at large does not have, then again we would be setting up a hierarchy for somebody to worship. That must never be.

Those of us who are in the teaching and healing ministry must recognize that whatever help we are giving to our students and patients is only temporary help, a "suffer it to be so now,"[21] a bridge, with the understanding that our students are learning to meditate to draw forth from within themselves so that they can go and do likewise.

Meditation Brings Forth the Word That Is Made Flesh

When the Master said, "Heal the sick, cleanse the lepers, raise the dead, cast out devils: freely ye have received, freely give,"[22] he was not saying that only one person is ordained to do these mighty works or only his immediate students. The real revelation is, "The kingdom of heaven is at hand,"[23] within us. The secret of harmonious living lies in bringing it forth. Meditation can be called "practicing the presence of God," because that is what we are doing every time we meditate. Every time we declare that the presence goes before us or every time that we declare that the place whereon we stand is holy ground because God is here, we are really practicing the presence of God, and it is that practice of the presence that eventually brings us the revelation of the nature of God.

It is through meditation that we ultimately realize how foolish it is to pray to God in the sense of asking God for anything or asking God to do anything for anybody. Through meditation, it is revealed to us that God is not a human being sitting around waiting for us to tell Him what to do and for whom to do it. Through meditation we learn that the nature of God is love. We might read that statement in scripture, but people have been reading that in the Bible for all the hundreds of years that it has been in print, and although many have accepted God as love, reading it in a book does not make it so.

To know God as love, we have to discover that truth through meditation; it has to be revealed from within us. Having somebody say it to us or write that God is love is very beautiful and may be helpful in calling it to our attention, but it is not going to demonstrate it for us. The demonstration of God as love comes when that is revealed from within our own being, when the voice within us says to us, "God is love."[24]

It is easy for anyone to tell us, quote to us, or point out that beautiful passage: "Be still, and know that I am God."[25] But that does not make us believe it. We cannot believe, "I am God," and we do not believe that anyone else is God in spite of what scripture says: "Be still, and know that I am God." One day as we meditate, however, that very statement will come forth from within us: "Be still." "Be still!" Then we have nothing to do with living our life:

> *I* in the midst of thee am mighty.
> *I* in the midst of thee am your bread, meat, wine, and
> water. *I* in the midst of thee go before you to
> "make the crooked places straight. . . . *I* go to prepare
> a place for you."[26] You rest; you relax.

When that revelation comes to us from within, we never again can be alone, we never again can fear quite so much.

Again Paul reminds us, "Neither death, nor life. . . shall be able to separate us from the love of God."[27] Is that statement going to stop anyone from fearing death? That has been in the Bible for all these four hundred years that it has been circulating and people still fear death. But if at any time something within us comes up and says; "Fear not; fear not, *I* am always with you. If you go to heaven, *I* will be there. If you make your bed in hell, *I* will be there. Neither life nor death can separate you from *My* love."

When that comes to the surface from within us, we have won eternal life. We have broken the whole illusion of death once that wells up from within us. But reading it will not do it for us. It is only when this comes through meditation.

My Grace Is Sufficient

Paul has given us the whole secret of supply and, since there are about twenty-five million copies of the Bible distributed every year, we must all be very rich because we have the secret of supply. With hundreds of millions of people reading that book every year, none of them should be poor after reading that statement because they all have the secret of supply. Yet half the world is underfed; half the world is undernourished; half the world is in lack and poverty; even though the world has been given the whole principle of supply: "My grace is sufficient for thee."[28]

That is all there is to supply: "My grace is sufficient for thee." What more do we need but that grace which is ever present? But reading it in a book does not make it true in our experience; reading it in a book will not demonstrate it. But if we ponder that statement and others like it, eventually something inside will say, "It is true, literally true. God's grace is my sufficiency." So never again do we take anxious thought for supply. When that happens within us, our demonstration of supply is made.

"The kingdom of God is within you."[29] The kingdom of God is already established, and all we have to do is to find a way of letting it out. We have to release the kingdom of God. This, we can do by the practice of meditation, even half a minute of meditation at mealtime to realize within ourselves: It is grace that we have food. We cannot grow food with money: it is a law of nature that grows food. We cannot grow trees and fruit with money: we can grow these only with the cooperation of the laws of nature. Therefore, it is not money that produces food: it is the grace of God that produces food—berries, nuts, fruits, vegetables, and all the rest of these things. Take the grace of God away, and all the money that we may have stored up in treasuries will not give us food: we cannot eat money. Let there be just a brief wink of an eye, a blink of an eye at mealtime, and an inner realization: "Thank You, Father. Thy grace has set this table." That is enough of a meditation to keep our food flowing to us regardless of what human conditions may be.

The teaching of the Infinite Way is that we have the whole kingdom of God within us, but we have to find a way of expressing it. We have to find out what it is that we have locked up within us that we are not releasing. If we are not being loving enough or if we are not being forgiving enough, if we are not being gentle enough, if we are not praying enough, if we are not acknowledging God in all our ways enough, then we have something more to do. Whatever it is, meditation will reveal to us what we have to do and how to do it. "There is a spirit in man: and the inspiration of the Almighty giveth them understanding."[30] "There is a spirit in man", and what are we going to do about it? That spirit in man is the spirit of God, and until we release It, It is not going to be a benediction or blessing to our families, our friends, our neighbors, and our enemies. There is a spirit in us. Let us learn through meditation how to release that spirit of God that It may go forth and bless this world.

Chapter Seven

Living Out From
Conscious Oneness

There comes a time in life when, regardless of what we learn, what we are reading or studying, we have to live our conviction; we have to live the life that is now unfolding to us.

There is a period in our experience when we may think of ourselves purely as students or initiates. During this period we are learning. We are taking in new principles, discarding old religious beliefs, superstitions, theories, and doctrines. We are learning not to be dependent on anything that exists in the external realm. We use everything as it comes along for good, but we do not depend on it. We are learning that there is only one power and that only a universal belief in two powers limits us. We are learning the nature of God. We are learning the nature of prayer. For the longest while, we are learning and learning, and learning and unlearning, learning to let go.

But then there comes a period when we must wonder what to do with all this learning. How do we go further than just continuing to learn? When we begin to live what we have learned, that, of course, is the beginning of our real experience and the purpose of all the learning.

One Life Flowing as Individual Life

The first great lesson on the spiritual path is that although we appear outwardly to be separate persons with separate interests, and humanly we live our life in that way, on the spiritual path we learn that this is not true. There is in the midst of us an invisible tree, the tree of life. This tree has invisible tentacles, vines reaching out, attached to each one of us, or rather, we are attached to this invisible vine that is attached to the tree. The life of the tree, which is God, flows out through the vine and becomes the life of us.

What does this do to us? It breaks down the belief that we are isolated individuals with a life of our own, because immediately we see that the life of the tree flowing through us is our real life. In that way we lose concern about our life. We need take no thought for our life because the life of the tree is our life, and It is doing all of the taking thought. It is concerning Itself for us. It knows our need before we do, and it is Its good pleasure to give us the kingdom. Always we see this invisible vine, with which we are one, and therefore, there really is not any you or any me to take thought for, because the only you or I there is, is the life of the tree. There is no separate life from the tree. There is the one life flowing as the individual life of you and me.

Only One Self

This is only the first part of the vision. Now we are beginning to see that we live and move and have our being as this life of the vine, the life of the tree. We live and move and have our being in the good that is flowing from the source. It is in us as we are in It, and this constitutes oneness.

> I can of my own self do nothing,
> but I do not have to do anything.
> The Father is doing the living of my life.

The Father is my life,
and because the life of the Father is my life,
the mind of the Father is my mind,
the soul of the Father is my soul.
There is only the Father and I,
and this is one, not two, one.

I am that place where God is individually manifested.
As I look around, I see all the other branches,
vines coming from the same tree,
all individual as individual you and
as individual me, and individual everyone.
No wonder the Master said,
"And call no man your father upon the earth:
for one is your Father, which is in heaven."[1]
That Father is our source.

We call ourselves American, German, Dutch, English, Spanish, or French as if we were separate entities. How nonsensical! We are all one. The difference is similar to the difference found in various fruits. Apples, peaches, pears, and plums are different in individuality, but the same life with the same source, enjoying the same food, the same protection, the same government.

So, too, when as individuals we begin to see that we are one with our source, we are one with everyone. We are all one with one another, because the same life-flow that is mine is the same life-flow that is yours. Then we begin to perceive why the Master said, "Inasmuch as ye have done it unto one of the least of these my brethren, ye have done it unto me."[2] In the whole tree of life, there is only one Self flowing out through the vine as our individual being, and so, we can begin to see that since the life of all of us is one, if it were at all possible for us to do harm to anyone, we would only be doing harm to ourselves. If we benefit anyone, we are really benefitting ourselves.

Oneness Must Be a
Demonstrable Truth

To read this and to hear this is one thing. Even to have a feeling within us, "Yes, this must be true," is another thing. The third thing, however, is to make this truth demonstrable in our experience.

The only way in which anything can enter our life experience is through our consciousness. Nothing can come into our experience except through our consciousness. In other words, if it were raining and we were not conscious of it, it would not be raining for us. If gold dollars were floating down from the sky and we were not conscious of them, they would be of no avail to us. If we had a big bank account and we were not conscious of it, it would be of no avail to us.

Nothing exists for us except what we become conscious of or aware of. Therefore, if we would bring the grace of God into our experience, we must consciously open our consciousness to the truth that "I and my Father are one."[3]

It is possible, however, for that statement alone to do more harm than good because it may give us a blind faith in a statement of truth, and no amount of blind faith in anything will help us. When we declare that I and the Father are one, we must have some concrete idea of what that means. We must either see this tree of life and its branches and realize that we are one of those branches and, therefore, it is true that "I and my Father are one," or, see the ocean and the waves and realize that as a wave we are really the ocean because there is no place an ocean ends and a wave begins. The wave is really the ocean itself in form. Somehow or other we must have the ability to understand how it is possible that "I and my Father are one," whether we use the illustration of the tree of life, as Jesus did in the 15th Chapter of John, or the illustration of the wave as being one with the ocean,[4] or any other illustration which makes this truth clear to us.

In some of my writings the example of glass and a tumbler is used.[5] Glass is really the substance: tumbler is the form. But how can we separate glass from the tumbler? We can't. They are inseparable because tumbler is only a name given to glass in a certain form.

God Appearing as Individual Being

The Infinite Way reveals that God appears on earth as man. God is the substance and essence, and man is the form. But in reality, man is only the form as which God-life is appearing on earth, God-mind appearing on earth, God's soul appearing on earth. It is God's way of appearing as individual form. Each one of us is the same God expressed as individual form. That form may make one person a doctor, a lawyer, a minister, a painter, an inventor, a musician, a composer, or an author. But it is the same life, the same mind, and the same soul, regardless of the form as which it appears.

Until it becomes as much a part of our life as breathing, we must specifically open ourselves each day to the idea of "I and my Father are one," and then follow through in meditation until one of these examples or a whole new one is made clear. God is so infinite that we could have a dozen examples that have never been thought of, because they would come to you from the same source that these came to me: from within. The within of me is the within of you. When you reach down inside of you, you are reaching into divine consciousness. That is where I reach. The divine consciousness in me is the same divine consciousness which is in you. Each one of us does not have a consciousness separate from the one consciousness any more than each one has a separate life.

If there are a thousand branches of a tree, do not they all reach back for the same sap? Are they not all reaching back to the same source? So would they not all get the same substance? When we meditate, it is as if we out here were just turning inside to the trunk. When we reach the center of the trunk, we are all in the same place. We are all in one place of one mind drawing upon the same wisdom.

At the Center Is the
Same One Consciousness

The question was asked of Joan of Arc, "When you hear God speak, does He speak to you in French?" She replied, "I don't know what language He speaks: I hear Him in French." It is the same with us. God speaks to us in the language of spirit. We may hear it in Dutch, French, German, or English, but God knows nothing about the language we are hearing. God is speaking in spiritual tongues, and we are interpreting it in whatever form our conditioning has built up since birth. We have been conditioned to hear in a certain language. But what we hear is the same. Why? Because deep down within is the same consciousness that is deep down in every person. When we reach It in meditation, we touch the same source that everyone else touches in meditation. This is the universality and oneness of consciousness and there is no other place to reach.

You can reach into consciousness, but when you do you are in the same consciousness in which I am. Therefore, while you may bring forth the same message, you will bring it forth in your language or with an example that is familiar to you. One person brings it forth in the language of a businessman; another brings it forth in the language that characterizes the message of the Infinite Way, which has been written in the language of Christian mysticism. All the Infinite Way books could be rewritten in Oriental or Hebrew mysticism, using the same principles, because the principles are all the same. The mystics in India, China, and Japan brought these principles forth in one way; the Christian mystics brought them forth in another way. But what did they bring forth? The selfsame principle: I and the Father are one; there is only one power; there is only one ego.

These principles are as universal as God is universal. They are found in the scriptures of all people, altered here and there by the conditioned mind of some of those who brought through the message. But if we go behind their conditioning, we find they are the same.

The Principle of Supply

Just as all spiritual wisdom comes from the one consciousness, so, too, it is with supply. We can bring forth as much supply as anybody who has ever lived. Whether that form of supply is of spiritual wisdom, art, literature, money, happiness, or health, it make no difference, because all good is embodied in consciousness and it has its source in the divine consciousness. To have it, we must bring it up from that consciousness.

When you close your eyes and go into consciousness, you are in the same room I am: you are in divine consciousness and you are bringing forth from the same source I am, or that Jesus did, or that any of the mystics or religious leaders who left a really worthwhile message touched. They all received their message from the same place. It came from within themselves where the kingdom of God is. All we have to do is remember, the moment we close our eyes, that we are like the branch of a tree looking back into the trunk of the tree. So, if a thousand are looking in, they are all seeing the same thing and drawing forth from the same source.

How the Infinite Way Developed
Through Conscious Oneness

There is another step we take in living this truth, which is far in advance of the illustration of the branch and the tree. This takes us a step further: My conscious oneness with God, with the source, constitutes my oneness with every individual spiritual idea and being. In other words, the moment I am consciously one with my source, I am one with the spiritual life of everyone on earth. No matter where anyone is, eventually those who are at this level of consciousness are drawn to me, because we are one. We have made contact invisibly and unknown to one another.

Then I have found that the strangest things happen. One person writes that he was in a public library and found an Infinite Way book and the title stood out as if it were in electric lights. Another one says that his neighbor had this book, didn't like it, and suggested that he could get something out of it. In the most unusual ways, such as finding a book in a bus, people have found this message. They come from every part of the world and end up in my correspondence file.

Without advertising, without soliciting, without going any place except where I am invited, all this happens from around the world and with people I may never meet. Yet, because I have found my oneness with my source, everyone necessary to my experience and everyone I can bless must come together with me. It must be not merely that they can bless me. It has to be that they can derive a blessing. And it does not mean only those who can derive a blessing from me, but who can in some way contribute toward my blessing.

As we blend and unite in consciousness, there is a going out and a coming in. It is not that I am sitting here pouring out this message in this Letter to you who are receiving it, but what I am pouring out to you and what you are receiving is flowing back to me: it is flowing back in love; it is flowing back in gratitude; it is flowing back in understanding. There is a flow.

Never believe for a minute that anybody is a funnel just pouring out. There is no God in that. The only way that we can see God is when we are aware of this flow, a love that has to pour out, but a love that has to flow back. The more it flows out, the stronger it flows back, just as the harder we hit a ball against the wall the harder it will come back to us. The more love we can pour out, the more truth we can pour out, the more comes back.

This must all take place in consciousness, otherwise even though it is true, it is not happening to us. As long as we are conscious every day of our oneness with the source, constituting our oneness with all spiritual being and ideas, the flow takes place.

This is the theme of *The World Is New*. [6] It was one of the very first of the principles that was given me to show how this work would develop. The universal belief was that it could not develop without an organization or without financial backing. It could have developed that way humanly, but there were not large sums of money available and it had no reputation. So it had to unfold and develop by my sitting at home and realizing that my oneness with God constitutes my oneness with all spiritual being. Infinite Way students in the business world, in the artistic world, in the medical world, in every area of human activity have proved the same principle. As they realized their oneness with their source, business flowed, art flowed, ideas flowed, or whatever was necessary to their unfoldment.

Drawing Forth From Consciousness

The Master never said that the truth would make us free, he said, "Ye shall know the truth, and the truth shall make you free." [7] It is not the truth that makes us free. It is our knowing of it. If the truth would make us free, Jesus would have been riding in automobiles, because the same truth about automobiles existed then as exists now. But nobody knew that truth; nobody had drawn it up from deep down within consciousness. So it is that there are great things yet to be revealed to the world. And where are those things? They are in consciousness, but actually they are in your consciousness and my consciousness, in the one infinite consciousness.

I cannot draw forth inventions because my interest does not take that direction, but they are there. If my mind were set in that direction they would come. I cannot draw forth art because my mind is not set in that direction, but whatever my particular forte is, that I can draw forth. That does not mean, however, that all the other things are not there, too. The person who is mechanically inclined will draw forth mechanics, but that does not mean that the same spiritual truth is not in his consciousness.

This must be practiced. We must know that when we close our eyes in meditation we are now in the same consciousness that Jesus Christ was in; we are in the same consciousness Buddha was in; we are in the same consciousness that Lao-Tzu was in, and anything at all that any of these knew and a lot of things that they may not have known are available to us, because nobody yet has drawn forth all the spiritual wisdom that exists in consciousness.

Once we realize that when we close our eyes, we are in the divine consciousness and are to bring forth infinity, we must take the next step and realize that we are not bringing it forth from or for ourselves. There is no plan in the divine kingdom that any one of us has a monopoly on good. Therefore, Thomas Edison could not bring forth electric lights for his home alone. Henry Ford could not bring forth automobiles only for his family. When something comes through it is universal, and we must be prepared to let it flow. There must be no thought that God sent this to me for my special benefit. We bring it forth from God but now it must flow. Always it must flow. There must be twelve baskets full to share. If we are not pouring it out, it will be like the fruit on the tree that just dries up and keeps the next crop from coming.

Attuning to Consciousness Must Be Selfless

The greatest barrier to prayer is to go within and want something for the little human self. There is no God that knows such a self. God is fulfilling and expressing Himself, and heaven forbid that it should ever be just for you or for me, because if that were true, He would be cutting off the rest of the world, wouldn't He?

When I go within, it should not be for me. It should be for the revelation and the unfoldment of whatever God has, and then whether it is for me or for you, let it come forth and let us share it. Always because the lesser is included in the greater, as long as I go within for the unfoldment of good without thinking of it as my good, much good unfolds that I can share but my own is included in it. I am not left out. But I am left out if I go within for me, or if I go within for mine.

If I were to turn to the center within asking for the health of my child, and if there were such a thing as a personal God, can you not hear Him laugh and hear Him say, "Why is your child better than your neighbor's? What is there that *I* have that is for your child any more than for your neighbor's child?" So I cannot go in and ask for something for my child. I can only ask for a revelation of whatever children need, and then *I* have it for my child, but I also have it for all the other children who may come into my experience.

We have been conditioned about the nature of prayer. We have thought of going within to pray for something for us and we have wondered why it did not come about. We must go into meditation or treatment for universal good:

> Father, reveal Thyself; Father, reveal Thy truth—
> not the truth about me, but the truth about
> all mankind and the world.

There is no more truth about me than there is about you. Otherwise God would be a respecter of persons. Whatever truth comes through about anyone must be the truth about everyone. Whatever truth comes through about anyone must be the truth about every individual person. When we pray, let us not pray amiss. We close our eyes, shutting out the outside world of appearances, and we are in the divine consciousness of being, in the infinite consciousness. Let us not go in there to bring forth a few coppers. Let a whole diamond mine come out. And if it is too much for us, then we share it. But let us not limit what is going to come out, turning within seeking something for some tiny little purpose or some tiny little person. Let God reveal Himself in His fullness, and then our needs are all taken care of, and we have the twelve basketful left over to share with others.

We Set in Motion
What Returns to Us

I have indicated that we must reach a point beyond the illustration of the branch and the tree, raise ourselves up, and stop thinking in terms of the material form of the tree. Our eyes are closed, and we are not turning within just for ourselves. We know that, having closed our eyes to the outside appearance of separateness, we are really in the consciousness of one another. We are in the one divine consciousness which is the consciousness of each other. Spiritually, not physically, all together in one consciousness, is it not clear that whatever blesses any one of us blesses everyone?

If it were possible for any one of us to harm another, he would only be harming himself because he is a part of that allness. This is why the Oriental teaching of karma came into existence. The evil that we do another we do to ourselves and it must come back to us. The good that we do to another we are doing to ourselves and it will, also, come back. This same teaching was carried over into the teaching of Christ Jesus, a teaching we know as the as-ye-sow-so-shall-ye-reap teaching. As we do unto another it will be done unto us.

There is no God deciding this at all. It is a law that we set in motion. If I am filling my thought with truth and love about you, that is what has to come back to me. You have no more power to withhold it than you have power to send it out. I am the one who sends it out, and it is going to make a circle. It is going to reach you, go through you, and then come back to me. But remember that if I send out evil, greed, lust, animosity, jealousy, envy, hate, never forget that it does not stop with you. It goes to you, through you, and around back to me. Why? We are not really two separate beings. All we have to do is close our eyes and know we are right there together in that one infinite consciousness.

It would be an utter impossibility to share truth, life, and love with others without its completing the circle. Round and round and round it goes in eternal expression. The moment we release any universal belief or any hate, envy, jealousy, malice, we are aiming it at ourselves.

There is no God punishing us. Never believe there is. We set in motion the law: "Inasmuch as ye have done it unto the least of these my brethren," ye have set in motion the law that will come back to you. "Inasmuch as ye did it not to one of the least of these,"[8] ye have set in motion the law that is going to come back to you. It is ye: as-ye-sow-so-shall-ye-reap. It is not going to bother your neighbor on either side: it is you. And it is not going to be visited unto your children unto the third and fourth generation. That is another lot of nonsense. It is going to come back to the individual.

Becoming Purified of Malpractice

While those who have already reached the stage of spiritual unfoldment where they are no longer indulging the world's degree of sensuality, envy, jealousy, or malice, there is a fault that is still found among spiritual students because of their ignorance of it. If we think of our neighbor as a human being, we are malpracticing him, and that very belief of being human will come back and make us a human being again. A human being means partly healthy and partly sick, partly alive and partly dead, partly rich and partly poor. Humanhood is made up of the pairs of opposites. Humanhood is made up of good and evil. The moment that we judge this world and the people in it from the standpoint of humanhood, we are setting in motion the malpractice that comes back to us.

Every day there must be a period of what I call *purification*. Many times throughout the day we express human thoughts about people in the world, but at least once a day we should sit down and purify ourselves to the extent of knowing that no matter what human judgments we may express or what human correction we may give anybody, this is only on the surface and is but the appearance-world.

> I know that you are spiritual;
> I know that I am you;
> I know that you are me;
> and I know that the Father is our being.

In reality, we know that there is no evil in anyone. But in the human experience of appearances, there are times when we must correct a person and sometimes in a way that that person may not like. There are times when we are bound to have some harsh opinions or judgments of people, especially those in high places. But underneath we are saying, "Father, forgive me. I know better. I am purifying myself consciously because even though I may have to indulge human emotions during the day in some sort of circumstances and with some people, inwardly I don't mean it." It is very much like a mother chastising a child. Even when she is doing it, she does not dislike the child, she does not really mean what she is doing. It is just a surface thing to make the child wake up.

So with us, even though we may have some harsh things to think about some of the people in the world, let us at least not mean it inside ourselves. Let us have one period a day when we close our eyes in a complete spiritual state of consciousness with everyone else there, too, everyone because "God is no respecter of persons,"[9] and we are all embodied in this divine consciousness.

Spiritual Purity,
a Blessing to Everyone

Just as one big plate of glass can be molded into a thousand different forms, so the one infinite consciousness is appearing as three billion people. Only when the eyes are closed, however, and we are looking deep down within can we realize: "This is the divine consciousness of everyone. Therefore, I am in his consciousness, and he is in mine." The fact that anything I may think about another person is what is going to come back to me some day makes me careful. That is where the purity comes in. It is necessary for us to be pure in our relationships with one another because the moment we let ourselves become too human we drag ourselves down into humanhood again. What we are thinking of the other, we are doing to ourselves.

Each one of us is intended to be a blessing to all the earth: the animal world, the vegetable world, the mineral world, the human world. But we are not being that blessing to one another except in proportion as we have this spiritual purity, in that, looking down into this consciousness, we can see that it is all the same consciousness. We are all embodied in this One. We are all deriving our life, soul, mind, and spirit from this One. We are deriving our good from this One. Then when we open our eyes to the appearance-world and see a person do something wrong we can say, "Father, forgive him. On the surface he does not know what he is doing. Father, forgive him. It's all surface." Out here often we are not aware of what we are doing, because, caught up in humanhood, we do not know our relationship to one another.

It is easy to forgive because no one is doing any injury or harm except those who are ignorant of this truth, and they cannot help it. They think there is a "me," separate from them, and if they can take a thousand dollars away from me, they have a thousand dollars and I have nothing. They do not realize that what has happened is that they have stolen from themselves. So, in their ignorance, they keep on stealing. We can forgive them because they do not know the truth.

Whatever an individual does out here in the world, he would not do it if he knew that he is the one to whom he is doing it, nor would he do it if he knew that he could close his eyes and draw infinity up from within. He does what he does because he thinks that is the only way he can get what he wants.

Putting the Principle of Oneness Into Practice

The spiritual student who is putting these principles into practice has to have a period every day to realize:

My supply is from within.
It is the infinite divine consciousness appearing
as form. Whether that form is dollars,
francs, or pounds makes no difference.
Whether that form is a house or an automobile
makes no difference. I am deriving my good
from my consciousness. That is the substance
of the form of my supply.

Let me give the first fruits to God,
recognizing God as the source.
Scripture shows me how to give back
the first fruits: "If a man say, I love God,
and hateth his brother, he is a liar:
for he that loveth not his brother whom he hath seen
how can he love God whom he hath not seen?"[10]

The only way in which we can love God supremely is in the love we share with man, because aside from man, where is there a God? God is the consciousness of man. Only in doing unto man are we doing unto God. Therefore, we share our first fruits any way we want to share them—the first fruits of prayer, the

first fruits of love, the first fruits of money. It makes no difference how, as long as we take the first fruits and share in some
way. We are then merely putting back into that infinite source
that which is moving around in the circle again.

The point of all of this is that the lessons we have learned in
the Infinite Way must be put into practice by us consciously,
because only what we consciously put into practice will come
back to us as a living experience. What we just read or hear that
goes in and out is very pleasant and is better than newspapers
and television, but it is not really productive of the spiritual life.

The spiritual life begins when we begin to practice the principles that have become clear to us. It is never good to use a passage of scripture or truth unless we understand its meaning.
There is a danger in merely repeating, "I and my Father are
one," or in saying, "God is my supply." Without understanding
the meaning of the statements we make, we are apt to think that
those statements are going to do something for us. They will do
no more for us than reciting the rosary or racing through a
recitation of the Lord's Prayer. Only as we go inside and con-
ceive of the meaning of "I and my Father are one," or the meaning of giving our first fruits and having it clarified by some illustration, can any scriptural message or truth-statement do anything for us.

"I Have Meat"

One statement from the Bible has become a major principle of my own life, one that I lived by and through to an
extraordinary extent: "I have meat to eat that ye know not of."[11]
That quotation sounds like a senseless one. Repeating it and
repeating it will only hypnotize a person. But it means something to me, and therefore, it has played a significant part in the
demonstration of my life.

"I have meat to eat that ye know not of." To me this means
that I am in an infinite sea of consciousness and that this infi-

nite sea of consciousness is the substance of my meat, bread, wine, water, love, human relationships, transportation, and all the rest of it. By knowing this truth, it appears externally as the forms necessary for my life. Therefore, I can share with you, and I can accept from you, but never will I say that I am dependent on you or need you, because I have "meat." I have the awareness that within me is infinite consciousness but not only here within me: I see It spreading all over the whole universe.

Scripture Must Be Clarified for Us

We have to take a passage, clarify for ourselves what it means, and then we can live with it. If we said, "God is my supply," we would have to know what God is. Then we know what supply is and we can say, "God is my supply," never looking to a human avenue again. How many foolish people there are who make such statements and have not the faintest idea of what God is, what supply is, what love is, or what the first fruits are!

The whole demonstration of the world-wide activity of the Infinite Way was made on the day it was revealed to me that the name and nature of God is *I*. It all came out of one unfoldment. Moses made his demonstration on one revelation: "I Am That I Am."[12] He never needed another teaching.

Jesus had only one teaching, the *I*: "He that seeth me seeth him that sent me,"[13] for I and the Father are one. *I* am the meat and the water. *I* am the life and the resurrection. "I am come that they might have life, and that they might have it more abundantly."[14] His whole demonstration was built around one word.

We think that we need everything that is in thirty books. We don't! If we catch one, two, or three principles, our whole life's demonstration is made. It is like all phases of life. What we put into it is what we get out of it. What we put into our study, what we put into our practice, what we put into our devotion, what we put into living the Infinite Way, that is what comes back.

❦

Chapter Eight

Special Lesson on Healing Work

Those who have not spent considerable time practicing spiritual principles will at times forget them, and thereby delay their experience of good. And what is it they will forget? They will forget that they are not to look to one another for anything, and that includes husbands and wives, parents and children.

The very earliest time possible in the morning, we open ourselves to God's grace and consciously realize that we live, not by might or by power, but by the spirit. We live, not by bread alone, but by every word that proceeds out of the mouth of God; neither do we live by the favor of individuals, or the good will of individuals; nor do we live by our place or position in life. We live by the grace of God.

Our Good Flows From the Center of Our Being

If we are to live in the mystical consciousness, we must abide in the realization that our expectancy is always and only from the spiritual source within us. We must abide in the truth that "I have meat to eat that ye know not of,"[1] and then be careful not to look to a person, a thing, an organization, or a relationship for it.

When we thoroughly understand and realize this oneness, as if there were only one person in the world, God appearing as individual being, our good must flow from within us, not to us from anyone, but from us and through us. Our good may come to us through people, but there is no law that says it has to. There is no law or rule that says we must derive our income from our work. Within us must be the complete realization that our manna can fall from the sky or, if necessary, ravens can bring us food.

Our supply can come through a thousand different directions. Therefore, we need not look to anyone. Of course, there must always be that sense of gratitude to those through whom it comes, but not the feeling that it comes from them: it comes through them; but it comes from the center of our being. *I* is infinite, and there is nothing and no one outside of us; therefore, all that is to be ours must flow from the *I* of our being.

When we realize that, we can be as free as we wish to be in sharing, and just as free in receiving, grateful for the opportunity to share, grateful for receiving, but never for a moment moving to left or right from our inner conviction that "I and my Father are one."[2] Our good is derived from that relationship. When we demonstrate the relationship of I-and-my-Father-are-one, we are in the position of demonstrating it for those who come to us.

Harmony in Relationships Through the Realization of I

What are the problems of those who come to us? We could boil them all down to personal sense. Personal sense means that we are accepting two or more persons. There can be a husband and wife; there can be parent and child; there can be partners in business; there can be capital and labor relationships; there can be all kinds of human relationships; and every one of them at some time or other can be the source of discord and inharmony.

If we are called upon for help, we have only one remedy: to give spiritually, and that giving is our realization of *I*: "I and my Father are one." That relationship is an infinite relationship, the only relationship there is. So we do not have a "me" and God, and we do not have a me and a partner, and we do not have a me and another person at the conference table: we have only the *I* that I am, infinitely expressed. Then when we sit down at the conference table, a unity unfolds, a oneness of thought, a mutuality. It does so, however, not because anyone has psychologized about it, but because someone has realized that there are not two at the conference table: there is but one, and *I* am that one; *I*, God at the center of individual being, am that one.

I constitutes me; *I* constitutes you. *I*, God, constitutes individual being. Until we reduce the relationships between everyone to one, we are still dealing with the human world and trying to patch it up. We can succeed temporarily, just as war can end temporarily until the beginning of other wars. For permanent peace to be established in our household, in our community, our business, or our profession, however, there is only one way. We do not have two persons in conflict with one another *and* God. Instead, we come to the realization that *I* am the only one, and when we are abiding in that *I*-ness, the infinite individuality appearing as two or more persons will be one: one in purpose, one in solution of a problem, one in will.

See Only the I Am

This embodies for awhile, a discipline, because every time we look out here humanly, we see two or more, and what do we find? This one has a will in this way; that one has a will in that way; someone else has another will. Three people can sit down together, each with a will of his own, and there is a battle. But the solution to it from the standpoint of the practitioner is not to have three people with whom to deal, or thirty-three. We resolve them into one by realizing that there is only one life, there is only one mind, there is only one law, there is only one spirit, there is only one will, and *I Am* is that one. So whether *I Am* is Joel, *I Am* is Bill, or *I Am* is Mary, it is still *I Am*. Then, we have resolved the situation to where we do not have patient, practitioner, and God, nor do we have three people or thirty-three people, each with a will of his own.

In a spiritual activity, we do not bring two together in an attempt to make them one. We realize there is only one to begin with, and the *I* of me is that one. Then we can say, "Thy will be done,"[3] meaning that *I,* which is the *I* of each of us. When Thy will is done, it is made manifest in all who are concerned.

In this work health is only one of the problems that comes to us, but many health problems are caused by personal relationship problems—unhappiness in the home, unhappiness in business—which work on the system eventually to bring about ill health. So let us try to see that every problem that is brought to us for solution involves reducing the appearance to one, and that one, *I.*

In our individual experience, when we are dealing with people and can realize there is only one will, and the *I* of us is that will, there is then only one desire, there is then only one interest. Within the *I* that I am, there cannot be conflicting interests, so there is no use trying to reconcile them. We do not try to reconcile interests because this is psychology; this is a human patching up of the scene. There are no conflicts of interest, because *I* am one, and in that oneness there can be no conflict.

No Formulas in Spiritual Work

The more we ponder the great truth of withinness in our meditations, the closer we come to living the spiritual life, because we are more able to perceive that it is He that is within us that does the work, that it is He within us that performs, perfects, guides, leads, directs. Then we must realize that it is not He, because that would mean He and you or I. The He that we are speaking of is the *I* that I am, the Selfhood, the one infinite divine Selfhood that I am and you are. Then we begin to live from a different standpoint, not from the standpoint of getting, achieving, accomplishing, but from the standpoint of being and sharing. Being! Nothing to come from without, all to flow from within.

When we are called upon for help and have an inner assurance or awareness of the presence at the end of our meditation, nothing further is necessary. If we find that that is not resulting in the added things, the fruitage, then we go further and see if there is anything in that particular case requiring a further step. There are times when no treatment is given, no thought is given, and yet remarkable things take place. On the other hand, there are times when we are called upon for help, and it takes a half minute, three quarters of a minute, a whole minute before spiritual realization takes place. But then there are times when we have to sit up all day and all night before we attain the degree of awareness necessary for some particular case.

There are no formulas in spiritual work. There are principles, but there are no formulas. For that reason, each one must take the principles and work with them in an individual way, and bring them forth as fruitage in an individual way.

There are many, many times when calls come, and it is unnecessary to think a thought. Instantly that feeling is within, that assurance. Yet how well I know that there are times when it takes hours and hours and hours before the necessary realization takes place. That may be for any one of a dozen reasons, but the reasons are unimportant as far as we are concerned.

The Human Mind Is Not Spiritual Power

What counts is this: "By their fruits ye shall know them."[4] If we are meditating, and nothing is happening outside—no improvement, no harmony, no sign of grace—we may be assured that we have not gone far enough. That does not mean that we have not gone far enough every time. It means that we have not gone far enough that time. The next time may be only the matter of the blink of an eye, or half a minute of meditation.

Healing work is wholly spontaneous. No one can ever write a formula; no one can use a treatment that he used this morning or yesterday. This work does not lie in the realm of the mind. One might pass an examination on the principles of supply with a score of 100, but could that same person demonstrate supply? Probably not many would be getting the fruitage of that treatment, because the treatment would be in the realm of the mind and human knowledge, and that is not spiritual power. Realization is spiritual power.

Healing and a
Transformation of Consciousness

If we can realize the truth of anything in a moment, that is all we need. If some particular problem is obstinate and we have to continue with it for hours or days, that is what must be done. There are cases that we work with for months. I have worked on some for years before a healing has been brought about.

I know the answer. There has not been a transformation of consciousness, and healing, certainly the healings of the major problems, requires that there be a transformation of consciousness, a renewing of the mind, a shifting from the material state of consciousness to the spiritual. But whenever that yielding comes, whenever we begin to see a difference in the attitude of our patient who has been a long time with a problem, and we see a whole change of nature in him, we will know the healing is close at hand.

Accepting Thanks

We have no way of knowing when we accept a case whether we are going to have an instantaneous healing or a long drawn-out healing. We only know that we are supposed to live up to our highest sense of treatment and realization. Probably that is one of the reasons I admonish students never to accept praise. I do not mean when a person thanks a practitioner that the practitioner should reply he had nothing to do with the healing. That is not quite the correct response. That would be like the case of a woman who was healed of a very serious illness. When her husband went to the practitioner to offer him a check in gratitude for the healing, he said to the practitioner, "I have just come to thank you, and I want you to know how deeply I appreciate your work."

The practitioner's response was, "Do not thank me, I did not do it: God did."

"Oh," the man said, "I was going to leave you a check, but if you didn't have anything to do with it, I will give it to God."

So, let us not be quite so absolute or modest, because we do have something to do with a healing. We are instruments and are dedicating our life to spiritual realization, so we can accept thanks, but not praise. Accepting praise and accepting thanks are two quite different things, because praise would mean that we really have a big understanding or are deeply spiritual. Nothing can be further from the truth. It is not our understanding that does the work, and humanly we are not quite spiritual, so let us not accept praise in that direction.

Instead, let us always remember that there is only One, and that is *I,* so we really were not so great in bringing out a healing, because if there is only *I, I* does not need healing. We can be thanked for dedicating our lives so as to bring out this truth, but we cannot be praised for our understanding, our spirituality, or some other quality that someone thinks he sees in us.

We do have a tremendous function to play in healing work. This is one reason we can accept thanks. If we are alert to the message of the Infinite Way, we will not concern ourselves with patients, that is, with the name or identity of the patient or his problem. But when we are called upon, we will instantly lift our eyes and realize, "This is malpractice; this is anti-Christ; this is hypnotism; this is the 'arm of flesh,'[5] or nothingness; this is a belief in a selfhood apart from God, or a law apart from God."

The Claim, a Universal Malpractice, Hypnotism, a Mesmeric Belief in Two Powers

We handle the claim as an impersonal experience. We do not handle it as a person who has to be healed or reformed. It is an impersonal appearance. "Judge not according to the appearance, but judge righteous judgment."[6] It calls for constant alertness never to take the person or the claim into our thought. We know that since *I* am the only being, any other appearance is a state of hypnotism; any other appearance is a mesmeric suggestion of a selfhood apart from God; it is a universal belief in two powers.

Let us not be tempted to go to God to use a power to heal somebody. Let us not be tempted to take a patient up to God; that is duality. Instead, we hold to the truth that since *I* is infinite, incorporeal, spiritual being, this that is appearing to us is just a state of universal malpractice, a universal hypnotism, a nothingness. Then beautiful healings can take place.

Not only did I learn in the very beginning of my work, but I have had thirty years to observe that impersonalization and nothingization constitute the secret of spiritual healing. God is not going to favor you or me because we are sick: there are billions of people sick with whom God is not concerned. God is not going to favor you or me because we are practitioners who obey the Ten Commandments: there are people all over the world doing that. There is no God to do those things. There is God.

The *I* of my being and the *I* of your being, this is God, and God is incorporeal, God is spiritual, God is immortal, and God is eternal. A treatment will not make God that way. Neither will a treatment make us that way, for "I and my Father are one," not two. The minute we have God, *and,* we are out of a spiritual healing treatment. We have to have God *as* individual you and me and ask, "What about this appearance? What about this sin? What about this disease? What about this unemployment? What about this lack? What about this unhappiness?" Then we receive the answer, "It is a state of hypnotism, mesmeric belief in two powers, the belief of a selfhood apart from God."

Healing Work Accomplished
Through the Realization of I

Let us take the word *law.* We think of how many kinds of law we have on earth. But there is only one law. If God is spirit, and God is law, the only law there is, is spiritual. We can break any kind of a material law, mental law, or legal law by knowing that there is only one law and only one lawgiver. The verdict may seem to come from a judge on a bench or a jury, but we are not fooled by appearances. No judge is deciding a case, and neither is a jury.

There is only one being, and *I* am that being. There is only one law, and *I* am that law. In that way we will find justice and in no other way. If we look to man for justice, we will fail; if we look to man for our supply, we will fail; if we look to man for love, we will fail; but if we realize that all is embodied in the *I* that I am, appearing as infinite person, we are all right, and we see that anything else is only the appearance.

We can do healing work. All it takes is the realization of this truth: *I. I* is the truth of being; it is the only truth of being; and there is no other. That is why, when the Master was asked by Pilate, "What is truth?"[7] what could he do but turn away? How can we say to temporal power, "I am the truth." It would be like telling that to a traffic officer, would it not? The fact is, *I Am. I Am* is the truth, and anything else is a suggestion of the carnal mind, this belief of twoness, or duality.

If we really want to do healing work, let us not think of the man, woman, or child who is involved, how long he has been ill, or the nature of the illness. All of that just perpetuates it. Turn from the appearance and realize the nature of *I*. And what is this appearance? The "arm of flesh," really a hypnotic belief in twoness, a mesmeric suggestion of a selfhood apart from God.

Every Problem, a Temptation
Appearing as a Person

The belief of the carnal mind is so strong that it operates hypnotically in human consciousness, but once we recognize that, it is nullified. It is not a disease; it is not a condition; it is not a person: it is a suggestion or a temptation. When Jesus faced his three temptations, he turned on the tempter, "Get thee behind me, Satan!"[8] He did not argue with the temptations. Do not ever forget that. He did not deny them or come to grips with them, nor did he try to overcome them or remove them. He looked right through the temptations to the tempter.

That is what we do. We do not care whether the temptation is a sin, a disease, a lack, unemployment, or bad weather; we look right through the temptation to the tempter, and the tempter is a universal belief in a selfhood apart from God. The tempter is a universal belief in a law apart from God, a life apart from God. We look right at it and say, " 'Get thee behind me, Satan.' Thou art the 'arm of flesh.' "

If we begin battling evil, we are going to lose the battle. If we find ourselves passing a jewelry window and we begin to argue with ourselves whether we should reach in and grab some piece or not, we may lose and eventually succumb to the temptation, if not the first time, then the second or the third. We do not grapple with the particular form of error; that is only the decoy. Behind that form of error is the tempter, and that is not a power. We do not have to overcome it. We have to recognize it as the tempter, a nothingness, a belief in two powers, and after that we are done with it. That is our treatment.

Then we can sit down, if we like, and rejoice within ourselves in our inner communion with God, and enjoy the presence of God. But always our healing work is done when we have looked through the temptation to the tempter, and when we have recognized that tempter as carnal mind, mortal mind, the arm of flesh. We can give it any name we like—hypnotism or mesmerism—only when we give it a name, we have to drop it, because that name, whatever it is, must mean nothingness.

I explained to a class years ago that we would be completely free of all trouble on earth today were it not for the misinterpretation given one word. One word in the religious world has perpetuated the evils of this world, and that word is *devil.* Had it been understood in translation, as it was understood in the beginning, that devil is not a person, but an impersonal temptation or tempter, we would all be free today and would not be grappling with sin, disease, and death. We would not be fighting alcohol and drugs and all the rest of these things, because we would immediately see what they are : devil, evil, or personal sense, and the nothingness of them would be so apparent they would be dissolved.

The only reason evil appears difficult to us is that it appears as a person. We always have to deal with a person, and persons are hard to deal with. I gave it up long ago! I cannot win when there is another person involved. When I want to win, I have to go into my sanctuary all alone. I can lick myself.

Laying the Axe at the Root

The whole of Infinite Way healing work depends on two things: Do we know the nature of God? Do we know the nature of evil? If we do, we know the nature of prayer, for prayer is knowing the truth, and we know the truth only when we know the nature of God as *I,* all-inclusive being. When we know the nature of evil, not the nature of sin, not the nature of disease, not the nature of unemployment, but the nature of evil; we know what is behind those forms.

We have always been defeated because we have battled the forms and left the substance of the forms intact. We did not lay "the ax. . . unto the root of the tree."[9] We lopped off a little sickness here, a little sin here, or a little unemployment here, and we left the old carnal mind right behind it, as if it were a power ready to spring forth in another form of error tomorrow; whereas to perceive the nature of the tempter as universal illusion or universal mesmerism is to see it as no power. We can even call it *devil*, as long as we will see the devil as nothingness, as nonpower, as impersonal, meaning without person: without person in whom, on whom, or through whom to operate. How much more impersonal could the devil be made than to give it a tail and cloven hoofs? That should take it out of the range of being personal.

In translation, however, they could not see it, so they made God and devil opposites. Even dear old Paul suffered his way through life by seeing the carnal mind as "enmity against God."[10] It is no such thing. The carnal mind is not enmity against anything: the carnal mind is an illusion. How can an illusion fight anything or be an enemy of anything? The carnal mind is purely an illusion, and the moment we recognize that, we are doing healing work, because all we are suffering from is the belief that evil is personal.

Knowing the I
and the Nature of Evil

There are principles of the Infinite Way which are unique to this message, and here are the two most important ones: the *I* and the nature of evil. That changes our concept of treatment and prayer, because treatment has nothing to do with persons, and prayer has nothing to do with an attempt to get God to do something; so it changes our whole understanding of prayer, treatment, and of the healing ministry. Infinite Way books read in this light take on a whole new meaning, as do treatment and prayer.

There is only *I*. *I* is infinite;
I is self-contained and self-sustained.
"I have meat to eat that ye know not of."[11]
I have bread, meat, wine and water.
I incorporate within my own being
all my needs unto the end of the world.
I will never leave me, nor forsake me.
I will be with me to the end of the world,
and *I* is the source of the divine grace
that cares for me.

Neither life nor death can separate me
from the *I* that I am. The *I* that I am existed
before *I* was born; the *I* that I am will transcend
the grave; and the *I* will accompany me
forever and forever.

Any appearance of duality, discord,
inharmony, or even of human harmony,
I recognize as the carnal mind,
the arm of flesh, impersonal nothingness appearing
as form, and usually as the form of a person,
or the condition of a person.

Impersonalize, nothingize! Let us never be satisfied with a treatment until we have disposed of the patient and the concept we call God. When we have done that we are left with *I*, infinite being, and then we can look out at the appearance and say, "Devil, be gone", and not fight it. Let us be sure, above all else, that we do not physically or mentally fight discord. We will lose. Our salvation lies in seeing behind the particular appearance.

If we look out at the world of human beings with human eyes, we see physical being. If we let our gaze stay there, we cannot help anyone in any way. We cannot help; we cannot heal; we cannot reform; we cannot forgive; we cannot uplift. The only way that we can lift a person out of mortality is to have the discernment to see behind the appearance and realize that *I* which is God, infinite being.

So it is, if we look out and see young people, old people, sick people, well people, if we look and see unemployment and all these things, we are defeated at the outset. But when we can look through that appearance and see behind it the fabric of error, the fabric of nothingness, the substance of all evil as a belief in two powers, a belief in a selfhood apart from God, a universal belief—not yours, not mine—then we are free and we can free others. But we must look through the appearance to see God, and look through the other appearance of evil to see the substance of evil: the carnal mind or nothingness.

Above all, we must be sure that we do not accept two powers, and that we do not go out looking for a God-power, a truth, to do something to carnal mind. It will not. Do not look for truth to overcome error. It will not. Just remember that truth is infinite, and there is no enmity against truth. Two times two is four; there is no enmity against that. What about two times two is five? It is not enmity against two times two is four. It might be enmity against the believer, but not against the truth. There is no enmity to truth; there is no opposition to truth. The devil is not the opponent of God.

> Now is come salvation, and strength,
> and the kingdom of our God,
> and the power of his Christ:
> for the accuser of our brethren is cast down,
> which accused them before
> our God day and night.
>
> Revelation 12:10.

TAPE RECORDED EXCERPTS
Prepared by the Editor

"Mind as an Instrument"

"Mind is not a power. Not only is the mind not a synonym for God, it is not an infinite power; it is not even a tiny little bit of power; it is not any power at all. Mind is an instrument, and nothing more nor less than an instrument. It is absolutely unconditioned in its primal essence. It is neither good nor evil; it has no qualities of good or evil; it is just an instrument given to me for my use, to you for your use.

"Do you not say 'my mind,' 'his mind,' 'her mind'? You could not say 'his God,' 'her God,' or 'my God': there is only one God. There is no such thing as 'my God,' there is no such thing as 'your God.' The mind is not you, otherwise you would not be saying 'my mind,' 'his mind,' 'her mind.' But you can say 'my mind,' 'his mind,' 'her mind,' because we have a mind.

"We do not each have a mind of our own. There is only one universal mind, and it is an instrument. . . . What a change takes place in your life from the moment that you accept this one universal mind as a pure instrument, a reflector of what you hold in consciousness. Hold a lie in your mind, and you will get two times two is five. . . . Hold truth in your consciousness, and watch the harmony that you bring forth in your experience. . . . There is a 'you,' and you are the important part of the demonstration. Your mind is not the important part: you are the important part. 'Choose you this day.' . . . Your mind cannot choose: *you* choose, and then you hold in your mind the truth, so that it becomes a reflector, a transparency for your experience. . . .

"The greater proof [of this truth] will come as you yourself work with it, and find out that you receive in your mind these truths. You hold these truths in your mind; you let your mind be the transparency; and then watch the reflection in your outer life of these truths."

Joel S. Goldsmith, "Mind Is a Transparency,"
The 1962 London Special Class.

"When you are thinking, that . . . process is not *you*. It is an instrument which you are using for thought purposes, but behind the mind and the body, there is *you,* the thinker, and mind, the faculty of thought. Body is the instrument of its locomotion. Behind thought, there must be a thinker, and the thinker is not a person: the thinker is God, the soul of man. . . .

"If I am operating on the level of mind or thought, I could close my eyes and say that your body is well, your body functions normally, and your body responds to this truth that I am knowing. The chances are that in some cases there would be healing; there would be benefits; and in the olden days there really were remarkable healings. It was a higher level than believing that the body determined itself.

"But from our standpoint of spiritual healing and spiritual living, where we understand that God is really the soul, the law, the life unto all being, the substance, and that mind is an instrument and the body is the outer manifestation, we have an entirely different process. . . in which we close the eyes and think no thought. I will take no thought for. . . what your health shall be. I will merely sit there, knowing that my mind is an avenue of receptivity. Receptive to what? The still small voice, that which we call God, the soul of man. . . .

"In that silence in which I have become almost a vacuum, a listening vacuum, always attentive, never sleepy, never tired, always awake, alert—remember I am waiting for the visitation of the Christ; I'm not going to be caught asleep when It comes—then out of the stillness, out of the infinity which is God, out of the depths of my soul which is God, comes either a voice, a feeling, a stirring, a release, or an assurance. . . and the earth melts, that is, error dissolves, disappears."

Joel S. Goldsmith, "The World or My Kingdom:
Law or Grace," *The Second 1958 Chicago Closed Class.*

"Through the mind we know, we become aware. With the mind we reason, we think; therefore, mind must be an instrument or an effect: it cannot be a cause. Mind cannot cause anything, and the reason is that I am behind the mind. I can think through the mind and with the mind; I can reason with the mind and through the mind. I can use the mind; therefore, I am greater than the mind. . . . Even as a human being I am greater than the mind, because a human being can control his mind if he sets out to do that, wants to, and is willing to study and practice. A human being can use his mind for a reasoning purpose, a thinking purpose, a contemplating purpose. Therefore, even a human being is greater than his mind.

"Mind can never be God. Mind can be the instrument of either good or evil. You can think good thoughts with your mind or bad thoughts. You can perpetrate good deeds or bad deeds through the instrumentality of your mind. . . . Mind can be aware of something good or something evil. Try to imagine God in that light, and you will see how utterly fantastic it must be to think of God as mind. . . .

"God is too pure to behold iniquity. God is light, and in Him is no darkness at all. In other words, when you penetrate beyond mind, you are in the realm of neither good nor evil: you are in the realm of pure being."

Joel S. Goldsmith, "The Function of the Mind,"
The 1961 Los Angeles Closed Class.

Chapter Nine

The Spiritual Kingdom
Made Tangible

As we grow more and more proficient in meditation, we will become more quiet inside, so that eventually we can hear the still small voice, which is the object of meditation. God is not in the whirlwind or in the storm; God is not in disaster or disease; God is not in the troubles of the world. God is in the "still small voice,"[1] and when "he uttered his voice, the earth melted."[2] When God speaks, our problems dissolve, whether they are physical, mental, moral, financial, or whatever they may be. When we hear the voice of God, our entire outer universe changes. The whole world becomes different after we have begun to receive impartations from within.

God Must Be Realized

The secret revealed in spiritual teaching is that God is not in the visible universe, except where God is realized. The Hebrew people were in slavery to Pharaoh for hundreds of years, and yet they prayed to God religiously and faithfully and to the best of their ability. But nothing changed their slavery; and God was nowhere visible in their experience.

When Moses came face to face with God and heard the voice, however, not all of Pharaoh's armies could enslave the Hebrews any longer. Moses, even without armies, without arms, without weapons, was enabled to bring about the release of the Hebrew people from Pharaoh, in spite of his armies. That was possible because Moses was able to bring to bear the actual presence of God, not praying to *a* God, but actually bringing God's presence to earth in human consciousness.

The Hebrew prophets at different times brought some measure of freedom to the Hebrew people, but the Hebrews of those days were somewhat in the same position that people of the world are today. No matter how many times they get their freedom, they go back into slavery in some form or other. It makes no difference whether we think we are in slavery or not, we have been for a long time and so has the world. Why? The same reason the Hebrews were in slavery. There is always an interval when there is no God realized on earth, and this entire century has been such an interval for most persons. Where and when the actual realized presence of God is brought into experience, however, evils disappear from individual experience.

Spiritual Might
in the Affairs of Men

In this particular century, we have been taught how to bring the presence of God into our experience, and because we have, we have been able to remove ourselves from bondage to disease, to sin, to false appetites, to lack and limitation. We have not been able to do it for whole nations, because nowhere on earth do we have a whole nation of people dedicated to God. If a spiritual leader should come along today, the people would most likely be against him, because whatever people are seeking, they are seeking for it in material ways, not spiritual. They are seeking to win their victories by having the most powerful weapons;

they are seeking their wealth by purely human means and also holding onto their gains by human means. Nowhere on earth today is there a movement toward God except what can be found in a few small groups.

These groups are not only in the Infinite Way. There are small groups of spiritually-minded people, but few of them can be found in places where they might exert their spiritual awareness in the affairs of men.

At this particular period, however, we are beginning to approach an era in which the spiritual might of a few, the "ten"[3] righteous men, can save a city. The spiritual might of a few will eventually change the history of the world. I do not believe that there is going to be any violent outbreak of a widespread nature, for the simple reason that there is already enough of spiritual power loosed in the world so that the forces of evil can be held back. We are nearing that age. Probably before this century is over, spiritual might may be so recognized that it will be utilized in the affairs of men.

God Must Show Forth in Individual Life

We begin with the demonstration of God in our individual life, governing our individual health, supply, happiness, and relationships. This then spreads to those who are led to us and they begin to come together in small groups. From this the circle widens and before we know it, a dozen groups in this country, a dozen groups in that country, and eventually more and more come together and form larger groups, until the influence of these dedicated groups will be felt throughout the world. Until we individually can prove that the hearing of the voice is the dispelling of evil, however, we cannot expect our relatives, friends, or neighbors to believe it.

In other words, there is very little benefit in preaching this message. The only benefit there is, is in proving it in our individual life so that one, two, or three may witness it and unite with us, and thereby eventually these larger groups will be formed. Each one who is on the spiritual path must be dedicated to making actual contact with the presence of God within to the end that harmony may appear in our outer world.

The only place that contact can be made with God is within us. It is necessary to turn within until we are so still within that the voice can say to us, "Fear not, I am with you." From then on, there is nothing to fear, because that presence which we have realized dissolves those things that in human life we would fear.

God Is the Demonstration

In the June *Letter*, it was pointed out that one of the barriers to our harmony is trying to go to God *for* something. We must never forget that there is no God that is ever going to do something especially for us or give us something, because God *is* the something. When we go to God and become aware of the presence of God within us, the health of our countenance is there, the supply is there, and the cement in our human relationships.

There is no use in going to God for any material thing. The kingdom of God is not of "this world." God knows nothing about food and clothing in the material realm. The kingdom of God is a spiritual kingdom, and when we go to God we must go for that which God is: truth, life, love, peace, wholeness, completeness, perfection. We can go to God for the realization of God's grace, God's presence, God's law; we can go to God for the realization of His son, the Christ; but all our going to God must be kept on the spiritual level because "God is a Spirit: and they that worship him must worship him in spirit and in truth."[4] The Master said that it is wrong to ask God for what we shall eat, drink, or wherewithal we shall be clothed. We are to forget those things and seek the kingdom of God. Then the things will be added.

Becoming Free of the Belief of Good and Evil

The reason we behold things materially is that at some period or other in our history we accepted the universal Adamic belief in two powers. Originally, when Adam and Eve were in Eden, there was only one power and one presence. But in some way or other—nobody has ever explained how—the belief in two powers, good and evil, was accepted. Because of this belief in good and evil, we are told that Adam and Eve were expelled from the Garden of Eden, meaning that mankind was expelled from his spiritual, divine harmony, and for only one reason: the acceptance of two powers, good and evil.

Once we know this, we have the opportunity of reverting to the original truth, that is, of clearing ourselves of this universal belief in two powers. Individually we can turn and ask ourselves questions about the nature of God: What do I suppose God to be? Do I think of God as a great power fighting other powers? If I do, then I deny omnipotence, because under omnipotence God must be all-power, and there can be no other powers for God to fight. Do I accept the presence of evil in a person or in a condition? Then I am denying omnipresence, because omnipresence means the all-presence of God, and if there is an all-presence of God, there can be no other presence: no evil presence, no negative presence. Do I believe that anyone on earth can tell God what I need? If I do, then I am denying omniscience, the all-wisdom of God who knows our need before we ask.

The Illusory Nature of the Appearance World

When we undertake a spiritual teaching each one of us must determine within his consciousness if he can accept the truth of omnipotence and omnipresence in spite of appearances, and we have all the appearances against us. Are we strong enough to look through the appearance and acknowledge, "I can accept a God of omniscience, a God of all-wisdom, all-knowledge, a God of omnipotence, of all-power, a God of omnipresence, all-presence"? If we can, we must credit everything else that we behold as an illusion, as some false sense that we are entertaining.

For example, somebody may hold up a diamond, a very good, pure diamond, and we, in our ignorance, may call it glass. That does not change the nature of the diamond. It only fools us, because we have not seen it aright. Again, we may see the sky sitting on a mountain, and we might say, "Let's not drive up there. We cannot get by because the sky will hold us back." We do not change the fact that there is no sky sitting on the mountain; we fool ourselves and limit ourselves. We may see railroad tracks coming together in the distance and say, "Let us get off this train." Our ignorance does not change the fact that the tracks do not come together. It is that we are not seeing them as they are. So we see this universe, "through a glass, darkly"[5]; we do not see it face to face.

When we accept God as omniscience, God as omnipresence, God as omnipotence, we must agree that anything that we see of an evil nature can exist only as illusory sense, like the mirage on a desert in which we see a beautiful city where none is. We know it is not there, although the stranger on the desert may believe it is there, rush there, and find nothing. There is no reason why we cannot begin, even in a small way, to perceive that if God is spirit, and if God is infinite, omnipresent, omnipotent, omniscient spirit, then anything that we behold that is not of that nature must exist only as a false sense, an illusory sense, and the result in us must be that we lose our fear of it. This is the *modus operandi* of a spiritual healing treatment.

The Healing Consciousness Recognizes the Spiritual Universe as the Reality

The person who undertakes healing work must have arrived at the consciousness and the awareness that God is spirit, that this is a spiritual universe, that God is omniscient, omnipresent, and omnipotent, and that every other appearance is but an illusion. The practitioner, then, sits back calmly, with no fear of the appearance, regardless of its name or nature, because God is here where he is, God is there where the patient is, because God is omnipresent.

> The all-power of God is here where I am;
> the all-power of God is where my patient is.
> The omniscience, the all-wisdom,
> the all-love of God is here where I am
> and is there where my patient is.
> All space is filled with the love of God.

> God is life; therefore, all space is filled
> with the life of God.
> The life of God is ageless: it is not young
> and it is not old. The life of God is not healthy,
> and it is not sick: it is spiritual, eternal, harmonious.

> Then this appearance, regardless of its name or
> nature, has no law of God to support
> it, has no life of God to support it, has no substance
> of God to support it. It is purely illusory in nature.

Because there is no fear of the appearance, no fighting, no trying to overcome it, it dissolves of its own nothingness. All it was to begin with was illusion, a false sense, which we have entertained because the conditioned human mind is constituted of a belief in two powers, good and evil.

The Nature of the Transcendental Consciousness

A spiritual healer must be an individual who has risen above the ordinary level of consciousness and attained some measure of the transcendental or Christ-consciousness, that consciousness which is too pure to behold iniquity and does not see evil as something to battle. The Master said to the impulsive disciple, "Put up again thy sword into his place: for all they that take the sword shall perish with the sword."[6] At another time he said, "Resist not evil!"[7]

The person who would be a spiritual healer must first have prayed, read, studied, and meditated until some measure of that transcendental consciousness has come upon him so that he can sit and look at evil in any form—sin, disease, death, lack, limitation, war—without a trace of fear, and be able to say, "No, thou couldest have no power over me at all, because only God-power can operate in my experience. This is not a reality; this is not a person; this is not a condition. This is an illusory, substanceless, lawless appearance." As the practitioner sits in that perfect calm, healing must follow, more especially to the patient who is not looking to God to do something to a disease, but who is really beginning to understand that we look to God only for the presence and realization of God.

Overcoming the Fear of Death and the Fear of Evil

We have put our finger on the entire trouble with the world insofar as it relates to us individually and to the world collectively. If we could remove the belief of the power of good and evil from our own consciousness, would we fear death? No, because there would be no power of evil to cause death. The moment the fear of death is overcome, a person has attained immortal life. It is the fear of death that perpetuates disease in us; it is the fear of death that causes pain in us.

We may not believe that we are fearing death, but that is only because we are ignorant of what is handling us. Why should we fear a disease if it does not lead to death? Why should we fear a little pain if it does not lead to death? Why should we fear anything on earth—a bullet, a bomb, or a dictator? Only one reason: it may lead to death. When we eliminate from our consciousness a fear of death, we have overcome the world.

There is only one way in which the fear of death can be overcome, and that is in proportion to our vision that there are not two powers, because if there is not evil power, there is nothing to cause death. If good is the only power, we have nothing to fear. There is the point. We are a "house divided against itself."[8] We believe in good, but we believe much more in evil, because our fear is far greater than our confidence in good: our fear of lack, our fear of death, and our fear of sin.

All human life is made up of two powers, but predominantly our thought has more faith in the evil than in the good. Why? We have judged from appearances, and we have seen more evil in life than we have seen good. We have seen more years of war than we have seen of peace; we have seen more of man's inhumanity to man than we have seen of man's humanity to man; we have seen more poverty in the world than we have seen wealth; we have seen more disease in the world than we have seen health. Therefore, judging by appearances, our confidence in evil is far greater than our confidence in good.

We Must Go Beyond Mind to Spiritual Discernment

The student on the spiritual path must go beyond the realm of the mind, because if we are going to stay in the realm of the mind, we are going to believe in appearances and, therefore, have more faith in evil than in good. And that will not help us. Our faith must be in the spiritual—not in the human good or in the human evil. We must be aware of spirit as the one and only.

The spirit of God is present where I am;
the spirit of God is within me; the Christ,
the son of God, dwells in me. Spirit is the only real
activity, substance, and law in my experience.

We cannot see or believe that with the human mind. There must be a trace of the transcendental in us before we can see through the appearance and acknowledge, "Yes, I have been seeing 'through a glass darkly,' because I have been seeing through my eyes." The Master raises the important question, "Having eyes, see ye not? and having ears, hear ye not?"[9] He is not referring to human sight but to spiritual vision. Do we have spiritual discernment? Do we have the spiritual discernment to see through ugly appearances, and see that actually these are only the product of a belief in two powers: good and evil? When we have transcended this we see:

I alone am power; *I* in the midst of thee am power,
not a power over evil.
I in the midst of thee am omnipotence,
the all and only power.
I in the midst of thee am omnipresence,
and *I* am come that ye might have life,
and that ye might have a life more abundant.

Freedom Through the Christ

This infinite presence that is within us is speaking to us: "Fear not! *I* am with you. *I* am come that you might have life, and have it more abundantly." We must rise to the spiritual vision where we can believe that there is a divine presence in us that has come, that has been placed in us that we might have life and that we might have it more abundantly. That has nothing to do with our age. It is speaking just as much to eight years of age, eighty, ninety, or a hundred years: "I will never leave thee, nor forsake thee.[10] . . . I am with you alway, even unto the end of the world."[11]

This *I* that is within us is the Christ, the same Christ that walked the Hebrew lands as Jesus, the same Christ that walked as Moses to lead the Hebrews out of slavery, the same Christ that was in Elijah, the same Christ that was in Elisha, the same Christ that walked with Paul and did all things through Paul, the same Christ that was in John. This Christ is in every individual since before time began.

The world has suffered because the truth of man's spiritual identity has been hidden, and the world has been taught to worship a Christ of two thousand years ago, and that has kept us from discovering the same Christ within our own being.

What happens when we discover that the Christ is within our own being? We are made free. Nobody can control us; nobody can influence us; nobody can take advantage of us; nobody can tell us that we have to burn lights or candles, or put coins in a poor box. Nobody can tell us what we must do, because we have realized our oneness with God and we do not *have* to do anything. Once we have attained the realization of the Christ within us, we are free. Nobody can tell us that our salvation depends on how many prayers we utter, or on how many communions we have or do not have.

When mankind learns of its freedom in Christ, it is free. After that, no one can hold anyone in bondage. That is why each one must learn for himself that he embodies his freedom within himself. That freedom is not dependent on others, any more than health or wealth is. Every good in our experience is dependent on the recognition of the Christ within us. Everything that is necessary to our unfoldment, to our progress, to our need in life is dependent, not on "man, whose breath is in his nostrils."[12] It is dependent only on our realization and recognition of the indwelling Christ and our ability to receive Its impartations, to hear the still small voice. All power—the power of what we call healing, the power of what we call the forgiving of our sins, the power of supply, the power of harmonious human relationships—all is in the recognition of this indwelling spirit that is in us.

This truth is not really a revelation of Christianity alone; this same revelation exists in Oriental teachings, only there it is called the Buddha. The Buddha has the same meaning as the Christ, enlightened One, Light. It is known in practically every one of the major religions that have been brought forth by the revelations of the great spiritual teachers of all time. Every one of these has this same teaching, that within man is the Buddha-mind, or the mind that was in Christ Jesus, and we must awaken to it. "Awake thou that sleepest, and rise from the dead, and Christ shall give thee light."[13] Awake to the truth that we have this indwelling spirit. How simple it is when we begin to train ourselves not to look to God for anything, but to look within and realize: There is no evil. There is neither good nor evil: there is only the presence of God, the presence of spirit.

Neither Good nor Evil

Our whole life changes as soon as we adopt for ourselves the truth that there is neither good nor evil: there is only God. There is neither good health nor bad health: there is only spiritual wholeness. There is no such thing as youth in the spirit; there is no such thing as age in the spirit: there is only the eternality of spirit, of life. The moment we begin to perceive that we are not trying to change evil into good—we are not trying to change bad health into good health; we are not trying to change lack into abundance; we are trying to realize only the omnipresence of infinite spirit—our life changes.

It is not finding a God that is going to do something to the evils that beset us. There is no God that is going to do anything to these evils, because they have no existence in any real sense. When we develop the spiritual vision that can say, "I cannot accept a God of spirit *and* evil. I cannot accept God as the lawgiver and at the same time accept evil, material or mental laws," then we begin to see. There is no more praying to God to do something, no more hoping that God will do something. Now it is a matter of knowing the truth that there is neither good nor evil: there is only God. There is neither good nor evil: there is only spirit. There are no evil conditions and good conditions: there are only spiritual conditions.

Practice Necessary to See Through Appearances

This begins a training program because, as we look out here, the appearances of evil are still out there; the newspaper is full of them. Therefore it is necessary to take a firm stand within ourselves and realize:

> Now I have learned that I must no longer fear
> appearances, no longer desire to change appearances.
> Now I must just sit back and rejoice. God, spirit, is
> omnipresence, and there is nothing out here to be
> changed, to be removed, to be healed, to be
> reformed. Out here is merely a world of appearances,
> sometimes good and sometimes bad, but I can ignore
> them both, because I know that the kingdom of God
> is within me, and the kingdom of God is spirit, the
> kingdom of God is life eternal.
>
> The Master said, "My peace I give unto you:
> not as the world giveth, give I unto you."[14]
> Therefore, I am not looking out here to this
> appearance-world to get peace. I am not looking out
> here to change appearances to get my peace.
> I let my peace unfold from within my own being,
> and it changes my world out here.

If we are still seeking our good out here in the world, we are not ready for the kingdom of God, because "My kingdom is not of this world."[15] The peace that the Christ gives is not the peace of this world. If we are looking to have our kingdom and our peace given to us by some change of circumstances out here, we are wrong spiritually. Humanly, it is perfectly all right; spiritually, it is all wrong. Spiritually, we sit back listening for an impartation from within:

> "Son, thou art ever with me,
> and all that I have is thine,"[16]
> all that I have.
> All that the spiritual kingdom has is thine.

> Thou art the child of God, heir of God.
> Thy good comes by inheritance—
> not by might, not by power,
> not by blood, sweat, and tears,
> but as a gift of God, as an inheritance of God.

"I and my Father are one,"[17] and it is because of this relationship of oneness that our good flows from within. Then when we open our eyes and still see evil appearances out here, we again turn within:

> I cannot fear, believe, or accept appearances.
> I know now that in seeing
> those appearances
> I am only seeing "through a glass, darkly."
> If I would see face to face,
> I must turn within and recognize
> that the kingdom of God
> is a spiritual kingdom,
> a kingdom of wholeness,
> completeness, perfection.

Acknowledge Omniscience, Omnipotence, and Omnipresence

We live in a world of fear. We fear weather; we fear climate; we fear bullets; we fear bombs; we fear men; we fear governments; we fear germs. We fear the calendar; each day it tells us we are getting older. Humanly, there is not much in the world that we are not fearing, and there is no way to overcome this fear but to accept God as spirit, to accept God as omniscience, omnipresence, omnipotence, and to agree that no longer do we fear "man, whose breath is in his nostrils." No longer do we fear mortal circumstances or conditions; no longer do we fear what man or conditions can do to us, because we know there is no evil power. We know that all evil exists only as appearance, as an illusory appearance, based on this universal belief in two powers.

Then how shall I pray and how shall I treat? This whole lesson has been a prayer and a treatment. It has been an acknowledgment of the omnipresence of God; it has been an acknowledgment of omnipresence, omnipotence, omniscience. It has been an acknowledgment that there is no other power but that of God or Spirit, and that is prayer. As a matter of fact, we have been communing with truth. We have been abiding in the truth and letting the truth abide in us, the truth of His presence, His power, His glory, and this is both prayer and treatment.

"He that abideth in me, and I in him, the same bringeth forth much fruit."[18] This *Me* is the Christ, this *Me* is the spirit of God. How can we abide there? Only consciously, only through our consciousness. When we acknowledge, "Christ liveth in me,"[19] we are letting the Christ abide in us. When we are not acknowledging It, we are denying It or ignoring It. But we must know the truth that makes us free, therefore, we must acknowledge, "The spirit of God dwelleth in me. 'I can do all things through Christ which strengtheneth me.[20]. . . I live; yet not I, but Christ liveth in me'[19]—Christ lives my life."

So it is that as we consciously dwell in the remembrance of these truths, we are abiding in the word and letting the word abide in us. As we consciously recognize that the son of God is incarnate in us, that God has planted His spirit in each and every one of us, we are dwelling in the Christ and letting the Christ dwell in us.

Loving the Christ
of Individual Being

Is there anything to fear when we begin to acknowledge that Christ lives in one another, that Christ lives in our enemy as well as in our friend, that Christ lives in the animal world, the vegetable world, and the mineral world? We cannot fear the Christ in anyone, and when we have acknowledged Christ in a person, we have lost our fear of him and we have begun to love our neighbor as ourselves. Who can love his neighbor, that is, the whole world of men and women, unless it is through loving the Christ in them? Certainly, we cannot love their human qualities, most of them; we cannot love some of the qualities of many of those who hold responsible positions in the governments of the world. There is only one way we can love them as ourselves, and that is to remember the Christ in them and love that, not love their human iniquity, not love their human incapacity, but love the Christ in them, recognize that they have the same indwelling Christ as we have.

Eventually, this is the way we are going to bring peace to the world. We must stop seeing men and women as evil and remember that the evil that they show forth is but an illusory sense, because within them is the same Christ that is within us. "God is no respecter of persons."[21] God did not leave the Christ out of the woman taken in adultery; He did not leave the Christ out of the thief on the cross. Be assured that He has not left the Christ out of anyone, anywhere, any time. But that Christ comes into manifestation only as we perceive It.

We can find this in our experience with animals. As long as we look upon them simply as dogs and cats, they will be dogs and cats. The moment we begin to see that there is a spiritual influence in them, the same as there is in those in the human world, only at a different level, they will begin to show forth their divine qualities. But we have to bring that forth in them. We have to recognize that in the midst of them is also planted the spirit, because if there is only one life, every animal is living the God-life at a different level of consciousness.

We Make Our Life-Experience

We really make our own life. The world does not make it for us. We, those of us on the spiritual path, make our own life-experience. We have the knowledge given to us of how to do this. The next question is whether or not we are going to use it. But we have the knowledge and we can make our own life by what degree of truth we embody in our consciousness, what degree of truth we live with day in and day out, what degree of truth we are willing to behold in our neighbor. All this makes or breaks our life, in proportion as we do or do not do it. If we abide in the truth, we bear fruit richly; if we do not abide in the truth, we are "cast forth as a branch, and. . . withered."[22]

We can watch how we begin to make our own life when we stop fearing appearances, go back within, and realize:

> All power is within me,
> in that Christ within me,
> in that omnipresence within me.
> I shall not fear the circumstances
> or conditions of the appearance-world.

We are united in this consciousness of truth. The truth that has been given to us, which is the word of God in us, is the power unto our experience. This consciousness is not merely a blessing to us, but a blessing to all those who come within range of our thought. All those we embrace in our thought receive the benefit of this truth which we have received in our consciousness. The more we keep this truth in our consciousness, the greater blessing we are to all who come within range of our consciousness, because whatever it is that we are in consciousness is what we are giving unto those who come into our experience.

This consciousness that we develop does not stay within us for our benefit: it flows out. That is one of the joys of the spirit. Nobody can save all the grace of God for himself. It does not know walls. The moment we develop some measure of this consciousness, it begins to flow out right through the walls to the very friends and relatives we embrace in our consciousness, and to the rest of the world which we embrace.

For this reason, a spiritual student has a great responsibility. Whatever is taking place in his consciousness is what is governing his household. It is what is being felt by the members of his household, his family, and neighborhood. Whatever he is not holding in consciousness is that much less of awareness other persons are experiencing in their contact with him.

Our consciousness is either full of truth, full of the substance and presence of God which is flowing out from us, or our consciousness is empty. If it is empty, when others meet us, all they can bump up against is emptiness. No one of us who maintains truth in his consciousness can ever be anything but a blessing to everyone who knows him. That is why our responsibility is less to ourselves than to family and community. Yes, that is why the Master could say, "My peace I give unto you." Whatever of peace and power we have, we are giving to and leaving with those who become a part of our experience.

Chapter Ten

God Dominion:
Not Man's Domination

The Infinite Way has accepted a God of omnipotence, that is, a God of all-power. While we all would gladly agree that that is the God we accept, very few of us, if any, accept a God of omnipotence as an actual fact. More especially is this true in this last century, since so much has been revealed about the nature of mental powers, the power of thought.

Attain a Conviction of Omnipotence

We, in the Infinite Way, however, not only accept and believe in a God of omnipotence, all-power, but we, also, recognize that the human mind and human thought are not power. To come into a demonstrable awareness of this, it is necessary to come to a point of conviction, not accepting it because it is written in a book, but putting it into practice, demonstrating it for ourselves, gaining an inner conviction, and proving beyond all doubt that God alone is power and that God does not give Its power to another. God is a "jealous God,"[1] maintaining unto Itself all power.

In this human world, which is cut off from God and is not under the law of God, nor under God's grace, anything and everything that we accept becomes a power in our experience. In other words, as a man "thinketh in his heart,"[2] so it is unto him, or in accordance with our belief, so be it unto us. As human beings, we can make anything a power. We have seen aspirin advertised as a cure for almost everything that exists, and at one time we even had tooth paste as a cure for consumption. I have no doubt that there are testimonies, too, to the fact that it actually worked, because if only we can develop an emotional faith in something or other, we can make it a God unto us, a law and a power.

Idolatry: Making Man-Made Creations Power

In scripture, placing power out here in form or effect is called idolatry. "Thou shalt not make unto thee any graven image, or any likeness of anything that is in heaven above, or that is in the earth beneath, or that is in the water under the earth."[3] Thou shalt not believe that anything that is man-made is power. Once we declare that the human mind or thought is power, however, we are taking a man-made creation and making it a power.

We might also say that we cannot take a God-made creation and make it a power. We have been told that only God can make a tree. If this is true, how wrong it would be, then, for us to worship trees and believe that they have some power over us. God made the sunshine and the rain; God made mountains and oceans. That is no reason for us to bow down to them and worship them, and believe that they have some power over us. God made the stars, and there are people who bow down and worship them and believe that they actually have some influence on their lives, and then, of course, they can prove that it is so. Why? Because they have accepted that as a law unto themselves, and it is so.

There is only one God, so there can be only one source of

power. There is only one God, and this one God is invisible; therefore, there can be only an invisible source of power. There is only one God, one lawgiver, one law, and God is spirit; therefore, the lawgiver is spirit, and certainly His law must be spiritual. When we give power to a mental or physical law, are we not practicing idolatry? Are we not declaring or accepting a power other than the one, the power of God, invisible and spiritual power?

A Conviction of Spiritual Government

Once we have worked with and practiced the principle of oneness until we have come to an actual conviction that God is spirit, God is invisible, that the law of God must be a spiritual law, and that this must be the all-power, changes take place in our life. From the moment that we can even intellectually agree that this must be truth, changes begin to appear; but much more so when through holding to this truth, maintaining this truth in our consciousness, abiding in it and letting it abide in us, we eventually come to that point of conviction, that point in which we say, "Ah, 'whereas I was blind, now I see.'[4] Before I may have intellectually agreed, but now spiritually I know and discern that God is spirit." Therefore, the government of this universe, the government of our individual life, and the government of our collective life must be spiritual.

We can watch this work out even in politics, where instead of putting our faith in the candidates for whom we vote or in the parties they represent, we fulfill our human obligation of choosing the candidate we believe to be best fitted and casting our vote according to our highest sense of right. Even while doing this, however, we should realize that the real government that is to come through these men is spiritual, that the real government is upon His shoulder, upon the Christ, and the real dominion of this world is the dominion of God, not the domination of man.

Rely on God's Government, Not Man's

If there is such a thing as right or wrong candidates, actually it would make no difference if we elected the wrong ones, if in so doing we at the same time realized that we were not putting our hope, faith, or confidence in the person, but in the divine government which will operate in and through him.

> I accept God as the only power;
> I accept God as the only law-giver,
> the only government, and that government, spiritual.
> I can trust God to exercise His judgment
> through the consciousness of individual man.

Such a realization destroys the power of the human mind and human thought and deprives an individual of the power to misuse the authority of his office.

When we look to "man, whose breath is in his nostrils,"[5] and believe that he is our salvation and look to him to run our country, our state, or our city, or expect the principles of a particular party to save us, we are subject to the domination of man. But if we can look behind the scene and acknowledge God—acknowledge God as omnipotent, acknowledge God as law and law-giver, acknowledge God as spirit, God's law as spiritual, and the government on His shoulder—we will elect men and women governed by God. Then our government will be conducted by men who are God-governed.

It makes little difference if those elected to office are religious or not, because religion is more or less associated with emotion, and for this reason we may be confused as to which religious teaching is true, and which is not. All of this would be of no consequence at all if we understood that it is not religion that gives us God's dominion: it is God operating in the consciousness of men that gives us our religion.

Eliminating Bigotry

We can go into any church, synagogue, mosque, or temple, and do our worshiping, and find that we are being God-governed. It would make little difference whether we went in with shoes on or shoes off, or whether we went in with hat on or hat off. Why? Because we would be going to one invisible, infinite, omnipotent, and omnipresent God. There must be just as much of God in a church as in a synagogue, mosque, temple, or in the hills or valleys.

Since God is omnipresent, there is no place where we can go and avoid the presence of God. If we mount up to heaven, we will find God; but if we make our bed in hell, we will also find God. If we "walk through the valley of the shadow of death,"[6] we will find God, because God is omnipresence. Then, when we have found God, God will reveal to us that "the place whereon thou standest is holy ground."[7] God does not say that that has to be in Jerusalem, nor does He say that it has to be in any city or any particular edifice. The place whereon we stand is holy ground if we will acknowledge that there is but one God, and that that God is invisible, omnipotent, omnipresent, here where we are.

When that happens, all bias, bigotry, and prejudice will be wiped out of religion, out of churches, out of the hearts and minds of men, women, and children. In the heart and soul of a God-inspired person, there can be no room for prejudice of any sort, because of the acknowledgment that there is only one God.

If there are individuals who entertain a particular concept of God and other individuals who entertain a different concept, and if there are some who lay down rules for worshiping God in a certain way, and others who worship God in another way; what difference does it make, once we have perceived that it is the same God we worship and that it is the God that exists wherever *I am* is?

The Widespread Influence of
a Spiritually Endowed Individual

There is only one way to free ourselves of human domination—whether it is domination in our home, domination in our government, domination in our church life—and that is to see that the human mind and its thoughts are not power. God, Spirit, is the only power, operating through spiritual law, operating in and through the consciousness of man. Once we begin to see this, we bring ourselves under the dominion of God and separate ourselves from the domination of men. Many individuals who have been victims of domination, through having been dominating, very often change or lose their characteristics of domination, and they themselves come under the government of God.

The influence of one spiritually endowed individual is limitless. The far-reaching effect of a Moses, an Elijah, a Jesus, a John, or a Paul is without limit. The influence of a spiritually endowed individual is not even limited to his own time or generation, but is unlimited throughout all space, all time, and in all countries. So it is that one individual, spiritually endowed, becomes a law unto his or her household, business, or community, because such a person brings the government of God into the very atmosphere where he is.

No person is spiritually endowed who is not under God's government. Only those who have submitted themselves to the government and the jurisdiction of God are spiritually endowed, and wherever they are, that influence is with them. In some measure, then, their spiritual enlightenment is felt in their homes, their communities, and sometimes on a wider scale, depending upon their own degree of spiritual endowment.

To What Do We Pay Homage?

It is important to understand that idolatry does not only mean not worshiping graven images. It means not worshiping anything that has form or outline, anything that can be a thing or a thought. Even a thought has form and outline, and a thought is man-created. When truth comes through the consciousness of an individual, it has power, not because it is a thought but because it has its source in the Word, and the Word itself is God, and that word becomes tangible as truth, the truth that is realized in consciousness.

From this moment on, let us watch to see to what we are paying homage, to what we are bowing down, and to what we are giving power, and then realize, "No, no, I can acknowledge only one power and that, the power of spirit through spiritual law, which has its source within me."

We are not talking about a God afar off: we are talking about a God that is in the midst of us; nor are we talking about some spiritual law that must come down to us from some place, but a spiritual law which is locked up within us, and which we must open out the way for it to escape.

Acknowledge the Kingdom Within

The kingdom of God is within us; the kingdom of spiritual law is within us; and we open out a way for this to escape and take over our life by our acknowledgment and recognition of it. The kingdom of the spiritual universe is within us; the kingdom of spiritual life and law is within us; the kingdom of spiritual intelligence and wisdom is within us. Our acknowledgment of this withinness permits it to escape and take over and govern our experience.

As long as we are worshiping an unknown God or a God afar off, it cannot function for us. Only when we recognize the fact that this spiritual kingdom within us is closer to us than our own breathing are we governed by the spiritual dominion of God, not by any domination of man, his beliefs, theories, or opinions.

We can overcome a great deal of confusion about religion and what religion may be best for us by looking at what some of the inspired leaders, revelators, or saviors of past centuries have taught. We, of the Western world, can do not better than to turn to the Master, Christ Jesus, and see if his religious teaching cannot be made practical in our own experience.

Jesus Revealed a God of Love

Jesus' teaching was a teaching of love, love for God and love for man, which he summed up in two commandments and which made unnecessary the other nine of the Ten Commandments: "Thou shalt love the Lord thy God with all thy heart, and with all thy soul, and with all thy mind. This is the first and great commandment. And the second is like unto it, Thou shalt love thy neighbor as thyself. On these two commandments hang all the law and the prophets."[8] His every action was a living testimony to these two commandments.

It is virtually an impossibility to love the God that we have known with all our heart, with all our soul, and with all our might, because in most cases the God about whom we have been taught is a very ancient concept of God, found in parts of the Old Testament, a concept which has been carried over into the Christian church. It is a God who rewards and a God who punishes, a God of damnation and hellfire, a God that seems to have very little patience with man, always finding some good excuse for punishing him. It is very difficult to love that kind of a God with all our heart and with all our soul, and at the same time be fearing that in the next breath He may decide to bring us home with a cancer, consumption, or an automobile wreck. It is not easy to love that God.

Before we can love God with all our heart and with all our soul, we have to lose that concept of God, and we have to turn again to the Master and see what he revealed about his God. There, we will find an entirely different God from the God that is taught in any church; we will find a different God than we have ever dreamed of, and it will be a God we can love, one, in fact whom we cannot help loving, and we will love this God with our entire devotion. With that God, it will not be difficult to be God-intoxicated. It will not be difficult to live, and move, and have our being in the God that Christ Jesus set forth for mankind, because this God is a God of love. This God evidences His love, not in punishing us, killing us, or ordering our execution; this God shows Itself forth as love by forgiving seventy times seven, by asking everyone even to pray for those of us who have been persecutors or in some other way devils on earth.

God proves to be a God of love by the ministry It sent forth through Christ Jesus. "I seek not mine own will, but the will of the Father which hath sent me."[9] The will of the Father that Jesus sets forth is: "Heal the sick, cleanse the lepers, raise the dead, cast out devils: freely ye have received, freely give"[10]—not murder people, not call them home with disease and accidents, not inflict punishment such as being stoned to death, or the age-old law of an-eye-for-an-eye-and-a-tooth-for-a-tooth. The God, Jesus taught is love, but this God evidences that love through healing, through forgiving, even unto seventy times seven, those who are instruments for evil in any and every form. To every one of them the message is:

> Come unto *Me*; drop your burdens at *My* feet;
> let *Me* take upon *Myself* your burdens.
> Drop these burdens at *My* feet, for *I* am love,
> *I* am forgiveness, *I* am the bread, and the meat,
> and the wine, and the water. *I* am the resurrection.

Our Sowing Determines Whether We Live Under the Domination of Man or the Dominion of God

Nowhere does Jesus reveal a God of punishment. Paul said, "Whatsoever a man soweth, that shall he also reap. For he that soweth to his flesh shall of the flesh reap corruption; but he that soweth to the Spirit shall of the Spirit reap life everlasting."[11]

This is not God: this is you; this is I. We determine whether we submit ourselves to the domination of man or to the dominion of God. We are the ones who decide. Are we putting our faith in material means, in material weapons, in material powers? Are we putting our faith in "princes,"[12] in "man, whose breath is in his nostrils?"[13] If so, we will reap corruption in our life. But if we are placing our faith in the invisible, omnipotent, omnipresent spirit of God that dwells within us, we are sowing to the spirit, and we will reap life everlasting.

The God the Master presents to us promises, "I am come that they might have life, and that they might have it more abundantly."[14] When we perceive that, how easy it is to love God, to worship God, to adore God, to praise God. Then we will know what a tremendous thing our individual life is. We will know how important we are to God.

When we hear about the starvation and the disease in India, China, and other parts of the world, and some of the injustices in the Western world, we might say to ourselves, "God certainly does not love His people very much. Why should I love God?"

Once we acknowledge the God that Christ Jesus introduced to this world, the God that he revealed is within us, love for God comes naturally and easily. When we accept that God, we can rest and relax, and take no thought for what we shall eat, or wherewithal we shall be clothed. "Which of you with taking thought can add to his stature one cubit?"[15] If, by taking thought, we cannot do even the least of these things, how then can we do the greater things? Knowing this, we relax from taking thought, from anxiety, from fear, and we relax even from a guilt complex about sins of the past, or even some of those of the present, and relinquish all these to God.

No Reason for Fear or Distrust of God

Let *Me* take this burden. *I* am in the midst of you. Drop your burden of guilt at *My* feet. *I* could forgive the woman taken in adultery; *I* could forgive the thief on the cross; *I* could forgive the boy born blind; *I* could forgive his adulterous parents; so *I* can forgive you.

    I in the midst of you can forgive you, because *I* am here in the midst of you that you might have life, and that you might have it more abundantly. Only obey *My* commandments: forgive those who persecute you; forgive those who wrong you; forgive them seventy times seven, even as *I* forgive you.

Does not the Lord's prayer show us how to pray? "Forgive us our debts, as we forgive our debtors."[16] We live the law of forgiveness as we want the law of forgiveness to operate for us. We live the law of love as we want the law of love to operate for us. Above all, let us recognize that *I, God,* is in the midst of us, and *I* am here that we might have life, and that we might have it more abundantly.

I am here to feed you
when you are hungry;
I am here to heal you if you are sick,
and to forgive you if you are in sin.
I am here to lead you into
the kingdom of God on earth.

In the God that the Master reveals to us, there is not to be found one single reason for distrusting or fearing God, not even for a second. We love Him, for His message to us is:

Drop these burdens at *My* feet. Let yesterday be yesterday, and let the past be the past, and remember that in any moment that you turn to *Me* within you, any moment that you turn to the spirit of God that dwelleth in you, in that moment you are forgiven. The fact that you may repeat some of these errors or sins a few more times is not of too much importance, because *I* will forgive seventy times seven, until there is no longer a capacity left for sin within you.

Disease and Death, Not God-Ordained

Let us learn the nature of God from the New Testament and make it some part of our daily reading. The Red Letter Testament enables us to read those words of the Master over and over again, day in and day out, until we can spiritually discern the message that he is revealing to us: a God of love, a God of omnipresence, a God of spirit, and a God of omnipotence. Thus do we bring ourselves out from under the domination not only of the men living today, but the beliefs and theories that have been handed down to us for centuries, which are making our lives miserable because we are accepting and believing them.

There is no truth, and never has been, in a God of punishment or in a God who ordained anyone's death, either as a punishment or by disease or by accident. "The last enemy that shall be destroyed is death,"[17] and it is the last enemy only because it has been drilled into us that death is inevitable. It is not inevitable; life eternal is inevitable. We begin to destroy the power of death over men the moment we recognize that death is not God-ordained. We, also, begin to break the spell of illness in our own experience when we recognize that disease is not God-ordained. Disease does not have its source in God; therefore, it has no legitimate father or mother. In other words, it has no real life or identity. Disease has no life, no identity, and no law, because it is not ordained of God.

When we can feel within ourselves some measure of a feeling of rightness about that statement, disease begins to lessen in our experience, because our fear of it lessens, and disease is maintained only through fear. We fear it and thereby cling to it, and even diseases that would leave us do not, because our own fear hugs them to us. We hug about ourselves the tatters and rags of our belief, and one of the most serious rags that we cling to is the belief that disease in some way has its origin in God, and that God, for some mysterious reason, has afflicted us.

God has not made us deaf, dumb, or blind. God has not touched our bodies to anything except the issue of divine life, truth, love, freedom, joy, and vitality. When we recognize that sin, disease, and death are not God-ordained and do not have their source in God, we have begun to lessen these in our own experience, and eventually in the experience of everyone who comes within range of our consciousness.

Through Spiritual Identity, Dominion Is Ours

There never can be God-dominion and freedom from man's domination until we understand our own identity. The spiritual nature of our being must be practiced by us until it becomes an absolute conviction because only through practice, can we inwardly discern it.

Let us go back to the familiar illustration of a tree. In our mind, we can visualize a tree. But we are not looking at the tree at all: we are looking only at the form of the tree, the shape of the tree, the outer shell of the tree. That which we are looking at is not the tree. The tree itself is the life that is flowing through that tree, causing the limbs to grow, and the buds, and the blossoms, and fruit to appear. The form is not the tree. The tree is the life.

Even as we look at a seed in our hand—the seed of an apple tree or the seed of a coconut tree—we are not seeing the tree, or even that which is going to bring forth the tree. The seed is nothing until the life-force begins to work in it and through it, and it is that life-force which is the real identity and substance of the tree. As long as that life-force works through it, that seed will become a tree, and eventually bear blossoms, flowers, and fruit, fulfilling whatever its nature may be.

You are not the form that you see in the mirror. That is not you: that is your body. There is a you other than that body. There is a you that possesses your mind and your body. When you begin to perceive this, the nature of your life changes, because now you can see why God gave you dominion and how you can exercise it.

Peace, Be Still, My Mind

Now close your eyes and voice the word *I* within yourself, silently, gently, secretly, sacredly: *I, I*. And now say to your mind and body:

> God has given me spiritual dominion
> over all that exists, and more especially
> do I have dominion over my mind and
> over my body. My mind must not be permitted
> to think any thoughts that it wishes;
> it must not be permitted to think any thoughts
> that are inflicted upon it by "man,
> whose breath is in his nostrils."
> My mind must be subject to God.
>
> Through my God-given dominion,
> I say to my mind: "Mind, peace, be still.
> Receive your wisdom from God.
> Receive God's peace and God's grace.
> Peace be unto you, my mind;
> God's peace be unto you, my mind;
> God's grace enrich you, my mind;
> God's life and God's love be with you,
> my mind. God governs you;
> man cannot dominate you."
> My mind is under the jurisdiction of God.
> My mind is subject to the laws of God,
> and because of the dominion that
> God has given me over my mind,
> I can say to my mind,

"Peace, be still;
God's grace, God's love, God's wisdom be with you.
Receive your life from God,
your wisdom from God,
your eternality, your immortality,
and your sanity from God.
The grace of God is your sufficiency.
God's dominion, through me, reaches my mind."

Assume Dominion Over Mind and Body

Think now how your body has been established within you.
I am sure that most of you can now feel that this body is not you,
but that this body is yours, and that God has given you dominion over this body. So, to this body which is yours, realize:

Peace be unto you. The peace that passes
understanding, the spiritual peace of God,
be unto you. God has given me dominion
over this body, and therefore,
I give unto you God's peace, God's health,
God's grace, God's strength, God's youth,
God's immortality. God's grace is your sufficiency.
You shall not live by bread alone.
Of course, I will feed you, and I will see to it
that I give you the most nutritious,
cleanest, and purest food I can.

God's grace is the substance of my body, and it is
God-governed, because I now bring it under God's
government and remove it from the domination
of man and the domination
of man's beliefs and theories.

To my mind, I give the best intellectual
and cultural food that I can. I do not live by intellect,
culture, or bread alone, but by every word
that proceedeth out of the mouth of God.

I remove my mind and body from the domination
of the masses and their ignorant beliefs,
and I place my mind and my body under
God's government, under God's dominion,
under God's grace.
To my mind and to my body
I give God-given dominion, strength, peace, joy,
power, spiritual freedom.
To my mind and to my body I give God's freedom,
the God-given freedom of the spirit.

My mind shall no longer be an outlet
for the mass mind, mass world, the carnal mind, or
mortal mind, for my mind is God-governed,
God-fed, God-directed by virtue of the power that
God has given unto me.
My body shall no longer be under
the laws of matter or the laws that men lay down,
for I place my body under the dominion of God.

Each day we call to conscious awareness this truth, even if
only for a second, to remind ourselves that our mind and body
are under God's government, spiritual government, spiritual law:
not mental or material, but spiritual. God's grace—spiritual presence and spiritual power—is our sufficiency of mind and body.

The Father says to every one of us: " 'Son, thou art ever with
me, and all that I have is thine.' [18] *My* peace give I unto your
mind and body."

We let the Master within us say to our mind and body, "My
peace give I unto thee, mind and body, not the peace that the

world gives, but My peace, spiritual peace, spiritual life, spiritual law." From now on our remembrance will be, not the domination of man, but the dominion of God. It is important for a while to remember each day,

> I am no longer dominated by man.
> My dominion is of God, operating through
> spiritual life and spiritual law within my
> consciousness. Every word that proceeds
> out of the mouth of God is the law unto
> my mind and unto my body.

This is the kind of a God that Christ Jesus has revealed to us. This is the only kind of a God that we honestly and sincerely can learn to love with all our heart, with all our soul, clinging to this God, not only throughout this lifetime, but throughout all lifetimes to come, because there will never be an end to the life of God which is our life.

TAPE RECORDED EXCERPTS
Prepared by the Editor

Every century and every decade present their full share of problems to challenge the wisdom and intelligence of leaders in government. This decade is no exception. So insurmountable do the national and international problems the world faces today appear to be that only a wisdom greater than mere human intelligence would be capable of coping with them.

This crisis in world affairs makes all the more important the world prayer work of Infinite Way students who dedicate themselves to a deeper realization of a government of omniscience and omnipotence. This was a function of the Infinite Way that was of the utmost importance to Joel as is evidenced by the following excerpt:

"Revealing the Divine Government"

"What is our duty in regard to the present world crisis? . . . This is a subject very close to our hearts in the message of the Infinite Way, and a subject on which we are working twenty-four hours a day around the clock, around the world.

"Our duty is to know the truth. It is more than a duty: it is a privilege, and it is even more than a privilege. Once you begin to see the fruitage of it, it is a great joy. As truth-students, this is a duty, and those who are not performing it are forfeiting a part of their own demonstration. . . because the greatest law of prayer is. . . to pray for your enemies.

"How do we pray for our enemies? How do we pray for world peace? Be assured of this: world peace is not going to come through the defeat of anyone, nor through anyone's victory. . . . As long as there are defeats and victories, there never will be peace. . . . There have been periods when nations have been heavily armed, and it did not prevent a war. There have been periods when nations were disarmed, and it did not prevent a war. . . .

"What is the solution? I have said to you before: the origin of evil. What is the origin of evil? It is the universal belief in two powers, the power of matter and the power of mind—whether it is the power of armaments or the power of tyrant's minds. . . . It is not always tyrants that bring about wars. More wars are brought about by ignorance than by tyranny. We, as truth-students, must pray daily in this way:

> God is the law unto His universe,
> and that which is not ordained of God is not power.
> That which is called mortal mind,
> carnal mind, the mind of tyrants, the mind of the
> stupid, the mind of the ignorant—this is not power.

God alone is power;
God in the midst of me is power;
God in the midst of man is power.
The spirit of God is power, and all this claim of
material and mental power is ignorance,
because there is but one power,
and God in the midst of me is that power.
Because of omnipresence,
God is power everywhere on the face of the globe.

"Praying the prayer of realization of God's grace, God's presence, omnipotence, omniscience, and the nonpower of the mind or matter that is not ordained of God, you will be fulfilling your function to this world, and you will watch the breaking up of error. . . and the gradual restoration of harmony."

Joel S. Goldsmith, "The Essence of the Infinite Way,"
The 1961 San Diego Special Class.

Chapter Eleven

Unconditioning the Mind

From the moment of its birth, a child's mind is being conditioned by some of its parents' beliefs. Much of what parents teach their children is fictitious and false, because the parents are merely passing on to the children the fiction they themselves have accepted as fact. It is much the same as the way many of us were taught about Santa Claus and accepted it, and our minds were, therefore, conditioned to the belief in Santa Claus. So, too, many of us have had concepts of God handed on to us which were almost as erroneous as the pagan concepts that were taught five thousand years ago. But we believed them, and our minds became conditioned to such concepts.

We have picked up political, religious, and economic convictions. From the moment of conception on, we have been conditioned to accept beliefs and theories that have absolutely no truth in them, with the result that most persons go through life limited by many of these convictions.

Unconditioning the Mind, Not a Psychological but a Spiritual Activity

When we live out from a conditioned mind and insist on holding to its concepts, we have no way at all of providing an entrance for the spiritual presence, or the Christ. Only as we begin the unconditioning process can we eventually arrive at that "mind. . . which was also in Christ Jesus."[1] We have to watch out that we do not approach this unconditioning process from a psychological standpoint, for then we would try to search out all the untruths we know, get rid of them, and substitute for them something that we consider to be truth. That way we could be conditioning ourselves with more fiction, because intellectually there is absolutely no way of knowing what is truth.

When we approach this subject from a spiritual standpoint, we do not try to discover which of our beliefs or thoughts are truth and which are not, but rather we accept the principle that spiritual truth is within ourselves and, as we learn to go within, this truth reveals itself to us, thereby revealing the unconditioned or pure mind.

Becoming unconditioned is not a mental process, nor is it a process of sorting out what is true and what is not and trying to discard the untrue and hold to the true. It is not sitting in judgment as to what is truth or what is not truth, but realizing that truth is within us: "The kingdom of God is within you."[2]

We cannot waste time by going back through our life to find out what we have learned that is right and what is wrong. The only thing we can do is to go within and be instructed by the Father. We are told in scripture that eventually "they shall be all taught of God,"[3] and if eventually, why not now?

Be Instructed From Within

"Truth is within ourselves."[4] At this very moment, all the truth that has ever been known is within us. We do not need books to find out what that truth is, although truth will lead us to books, books which we will use for a different purpose. "Truth is within ourselves," and all of the truth. "Son, thou art ever with me, and all that I have is thine."[5] All that the Father has of truth, all that the Father has of love, life, wisdom, all that is ours. It is within us, all given to us as a gift of God. We must know that this is the truth about all the people of the world. We cannot claim that truth as an exclusive inheritance, or else we would have to set up a new religion with a new figure above us, one who would eventually be crucified.

This should not happen in this enlightened age, for we do know that the kingdom of God is within us and that all that the Father has is ours. I have watched this operate in the consciousness of many students of the Infinite Way. I have watched how, as they opened themselves to the withinness, the kingdom within themselves, ideas began pouring out. Some were ideas of truth but, in other cases, music, art, literature, inventions, and discoveries were brought forth, and in some cases, hidden talents. It is all locked up within, waiting to be released.

"Son, thou art ever with me." This is true because I and the Father are one, and not two. Therefore, if I and the Father are one, all that the Father is, I am, and all that the Father has is mine. I must open out a way for this "imprisoned splendor"[6] to escape.

When we turn within in meditation, not for the purpose of using God, or truth, but for the purpose of being taught of God, eventually we come to that place of stillness, quietness, and confidence in which and through which truth begins to appear. All that has been written in the Infinite Way has come from within. A person is not born knowing that, and a great deal of it has certainly not been written before, so it would have to have come from within.

All artistic achievement, whether in music, painting, sculpture, or architecture, must come from within, but it comes only in proportion to our ability to listen and to be still. In that stillness, the mind becomes unconditioned of its beliefs, its theories, its false ideas, its misconceptions and misperceptions, and instead of thinking along the lines that we have followed heretofore, we begin to perceive new ideas, new thoughts, new truths coming into expression.

The Importance of
Creating a Vacuum Within

As human beings, we have been conditioned in our thinking, most of it through false teaching, and even if we spent three, four, or five years on a psychiatrist's couch, we still would not be able to tell him all the lies that are stored up in us. It would seem, therefore, that we would be better off to save that time and make the acknowledgment right now: "So much of what I know is not true. Let me ignore that; and, Father, enlighten me. 'Speak, Lord; for thy servant heareth.'"[7] We are then emptying out the vessel, making room for something new. When that something new appears, we quickly recognize that it is the presence of God or the Christ.

The ideal of spiritual living is to arrive at that place which Paul mentions: "I live; yet not I, but Christ liveth in me."[8] No person can rightly claim that, even in a degree, however, until an experience takes place whereby he knows that he is no longer living on his own powers, knowledge, influence, or station in life, but that now something from within has taken over and becomes the presence that goes before him to "make the crooked places straight."[9]

We, ourselves, are the barriers preventing this from happening because we do not create this vacuum into which the Christ can appear. We do not realize that there is no use going into meditation with made-up statements of truth. The statements may be true enough, and certainly, if we are quoting any of the mystics, we are quoting truth, but that is not the same as receiving truth from within.

Let God Utter His Voice

There is considerable difference between talking about God and experiencing God, between meditating and just thinking thoughts about God, and between meditating and being still enough so that God can utter His voice. When He utters His voice, the earth melts.[10] God is not in the whirlwind; God is not in the problem; and there is no use taking our problem into our thought, because there will not be any God in it, for God is in the "still small voice."[11]

As we go into meditation, into our period of prayer, communion, or treatment, we do not go in with a conditioned mind, not even one that is conditioned to make statements of truth. Rather, we go in with a pure mind that is receptive and responsive to the presence of God that is within us. It is a simple matter in going into meditation to remember:

> The kingdom of God is within me.
> The presence of God is within me,
> and the purpose of my being here is to let that voice
> thunder, let that still small voice come forth.

To realize that much alone makes it easy to meditate and to wait, even if it is only for sixty seconds.

To Keep From Mentalizing, Meditate Briefly But Frequently

Some of our students, however, wait in meditation for too long a period, or they meditate for too long at one time until meditation becomes a mental practice instead of a spiritual awareness. It is far better, when we sit down to meditate, to realize:

> The kingdom of God is within me now.
> The kingdom of God can reveal itself to me
> as I listen. That still small voice is within me
> and can utter Itself, and so my function is
> just to be here, be still, and let It.

If we can wait only twenty seconds in complete stillness, that is enough. The fact that we do not get a response means nothing. We do not need a response. We are not trying to satisfy the intellect: we are trying, through the unconditioned mind, to be a state of receptivity to the truth that is within us. If we practice doing this three, four, five, six, or ten times a day, even if for only twenty seconds, eventually we begin to increase in depth of listening, in depth of silence, and in depth of unconditioning, and we surprise ourselves by discovering after a while that we have been a whole minute, even two or three minutes in a meditation without having to have a mental exercise going on.

Patience! Patience!

It does require patience; it does require practice. The best practice we can have is to realize that this presence is within us. It makes no difference whether we are in a church or out, the place whereon we stand is holy ground. God is just as much down in a coal mine as in the kitchen. It makes no difference where we are, but we must be still long enough to give this presence a chance to express Itself. If we can be still for only ten, fifteen, or twenty seconds, we have begun the process of unconditioning, emptying out, and creating a vacuum. Then one of these days, when we are not really expecting it, the experience will be ours.

Sometimes we are too eager for the God-experience and we want to have it right away. We forget that we have had generations behind us that have made it difficult, if not almost impossible, for us really to get back to the kingdom of God, and we have to be patient with ourselves until we do reach that state of consciousness. It will not be too late; it will never be too late; but we have to begin, and we have to be patient.

Meditation: to Lift Us to Another Dimension of Consciousness

It is important, also, to know what we are doing. We go into meditation to receive the presence and the power of God. We know that we do not have to tell God about our problem. We do not have to explain to God that it is the right knee or the left foot. We do not have to explain to God that it is a problem of business, finance, or government. None of that! We have to go within only to experience the presence of God. The presence of God is the power of God, and where the presence of God is, there is no evil. When we have experienced the presence of God, whatever the discord may have been, whatever the nature of the appearance—mental, moral, physical, or financial—it evaporates.

To our human sense, we think of it as an overcoming of error, but it really is not, because there are not two powers. There is not a power overcoming another power. When Jesus said, "I have overcome the world,"[12] he did not mean that he had overcome the Hebrew synagogue, and he certainly had not overcome Caesar. He had not overcome the external world at all. He overcame the world-consciousness within himself, the material consciousness, the belief in two powers, the belief in good and evil. He had overcome within himself the this-world-consciousness, and was able to say, "My kingdom is not of this world,"[13] because he had overcome "this world" within himself. He no longer accepted two powers; he no longer had to work against one power to overcome it, because he had overcome the consciousness of duality within himself. He no longer had a spiritual universe and a material universe. He no longer had spiritual power and material power. He no longer had health and disease.

In our early life in metaphysics, and many times even on the spiritual path, we think in terms of getting rid of our discords and taking on harmony. We think of getting rid of disease and having health, or getting rid of lack and having abundance. All we are doing, really, is trying to exchange one material condition for another. One condition might be that of a dollar a day income, but after our metaphysical demonstration we have five; or it might be a condition of a bad heart, and then after our metaphysical experience we have a good heart. All of this is alright in our early stages, where we are merely exchanging the erroneous sense of this world for a more harmonious sense of this world.

As we go along on the spiritual path, we discover that if we had all the health we had dreamed about, we still might not have found inner peace or harmony. Furthermore, we discover how many healthy people there are who are not happy, contented, or at peace. In the same way, after we have dreamed about how glorious it will be when we are prosperous, and then find ourselves prosperous and still miserable, we begin to wonder. Evidently health is not really the solution to life or abundance. There is more to life than just health, abundance, and happiness. What is it?

Then is when we begin to take the really progressive steps on the spiritual path. We learn that there is a kingdom that is not of this world, that there is something far beyond health, something far beyond wealth, something far beyond happiness; but we are not going to experience it while we are merely trying to exchange one type of physical condition for another. It is only when we begin to take no thought for our life, for our food, clothing, or shelter, that we begin to realize that there is a spiritual kingdom, which is not of this world.

Through Contemplation of "My Peace," We Reach Another Realm

A passage of scripture, comes to our attention: "My peace I give unto you: not as the world giveth, give I unto you."[14] Now we have material for days and weeks ahead for contemplation:

What is *My* peace?
What is this peace that passes understanding?
What is this peace that the world cannot give?

The world can give me health; the world can give me

wealth, honor, fame, homes, palaces.
But what is *My* peace, spiritual peace?
It must be something that emanates from God;
something that is the direct gift of God to His son,
something which, when I have it,
I have all the other things added,
but if I do not have it,
and I have all the other things, I have nothing.

This peace "which passeth all understanding"[15] is in
the kingdom of God,
and therefore, it is also within me.
I am not coming to you for truth,
Father. I am not coming for the change
of any circumstance or condition in my life.
I have overcome the world and
the desire for anything in this world.
Now I am seeking Thy peace.

Thy grace, God's grace, is my sufficiency.
So I ask not for supply, for safety, or for security.
I ask just for Thy grace. What is this
"Thy grace" that is the sufficiency in all things?

With this meditation, we are in a new kingdom, in another realm. We are out of this world. We have overcome this world. How unconditioned we are in thinking when we are not seeking anything of this world! In our mind we have lost the mesmeric desire for person, place, thing, circumstance, or condition. We have lost in our mind any further seeking for fame, fortune, or glory. We have overcome that world, and now we are in the realm of the real, in the kingdom of God.

This is the son of God that I am. Now am I the son
of God. Because God is spirit, my whole mind,

being, and body are engaged in spiritual pursuits.
"I have overcome the world."
I am no longer the son of man, but the son of God.

My whole longing is for the things of God,
the thoughts of God, the ways of God,
and the will of God, that I may know Thee,
whom to know is life eternal.
Where Thou art, Father, I long to be.
In Thy house are many mansions;
in Thy kingdom is peace to be found,
the spiritual peace the world cannot give,
the only peace, because now it is not
Thy peace for the sake of material good:
it is Thy peace alone.

Thy grace is my sufficiency in all things.
When I have Thy grace,
I have all that is necessary to my experience.

When we no longer take thought for the things of this world and are abiding in His grace, the necessary food appears, the clothing, the harmony, the friends, or whatever is necessary in the human world, even if "the ravens"[16] have to bring it, even if the poor "widow"[17] has to share it. In one way or another, all things appear, but now without taking thought. No longer are we in the kingdom of this world: now we are in the kingdom of His grace; we are living in His presence, and there is no room in the mind for matter, no desire for matter, material things, material activities, or degrees of matter. This has all disappeared.

The Unconditioned Mind Knows No Longings

The unconditioned mind has in it no material concepts, longings, or desires. It is entirely an abiding place for the spirit of God. "Know ye not that ye are the temple of God, and that the Spirit of God dwelleth in you?"[18] Our mind is that temple of God, our unconditioned mind, the mind that no longer desires any *thing,* that desires only to know God's peace, God's grace, God's will. God's will! We enter into this new dimension where we have no will of our own, but we follow His leading when His will is made manifest in us, when His will is expressed in us, and we merely carry it out. Then we have made a transition from this world to "My kingdom." In the unconditioned mind there are no material thoughts.

> The kingdom of God is within me.
> The spirit of God dwells in me.
> I know that the spirit of God
> cannot dwell in me while I am thinking
> in terms of this world,
> but I have overcome this world.
> I have no more thoughts about
> wanting God
> for some worldly purpose.
> Now my mind is unconditioned and
> seeks only His peace, His grace, His will.

Seek Grace for No Purpose

This brings to light the great mystery that we have no life of our own. The life of God has become our life, because we are not thinking in terms of time or space; we are thinking in terms of eternity. In this spirit we live, and yet we have no feeling of age; we have no feeling of a physical body. We have overcome that world of physicality.

"For as many as are led by the spirit of God, they are the sons of God. . . . The Spirit itself beareth witness with our spirit, that we are the children of God: And if children, then heirs; heirs of God, and joint-heirs with Christ."[19] We bring this spirit of God into active expression when we do not want It for a purpose. We have overcome the world when we want the spirit of God, but not for a purpose.

> The spirit of God dwells in me
> when I seek It for Itself. Thy grace,
> Thy presence is my sufficiency in all things.
> I seek only Thy presence, but not for a reason,
> not for a purpose. I do not want to use It,
> just tabernacle with It, commune with It.

We have overcome the world in any moment in which we seek the grace of God, not for a healing, nor for supply, not to make the world better, but in our meditation to retire from this world and enter the kingdom of grace, enter the realm where we do not live by might or by power, where we do not use the sword, because we are not trying to hold onto anything material. The grace which is our sufficiency is the Christ, the son of God. This is the overcoming of this world: "My grace,"[20] for no reason, for no purpose.

It is in this kingdom of God where the voice speaks:

> Fear not, for *I* am with thee.
> *I* will be with thee unto the end of the world.
> Do not seek for bread, meat, wine,
> for *I* am thy bread, meat, wine, and water.
> Do not seek for any power of resurrection or healing,
> for *I* am the resurrection.

The Unconditioned Mind Abides In the Consciousness of the Presence

In this unconditioned mind, there is no movement toward attaining, achieving, or demonstrating anything. There is no movement of the mind outside of itself. There is an inner peace and an inner stillness, an abiding in Him:

I live and move and have my being in Him.
"I have overcome the world."
The world out here has dropped away,
and I have no concern for it,
for I am living and moving and having
my being in Him.

I am dwelling in Him, dwelling in His spirit,
and His spirit is dwelling in me, for we are one,
and there is no thought taking place
for an outside universe,
no thought taking place for an outside place,
for an outside person,
not even for the purpose of blessing him.
Even that has dropped away.
I am here, like a ball, all rolled up inside of myself,
like the statue of the hand of God,
with the man all folded up inside of that hand.

That is what takes place. Living and moving in Him, there is no outside world, and yet just as Jesus was abiding in this very consciousness of the Father, everyone who touched the hem of his robe was blessed. He was not thinking of blessing them, he had overcome this world. He was not thinking of feeding, housing, or healing them: he was abiding in his consciousness of God's presence, and then everyone who touched him, everyone who entered the realm of his atmosphere or aura physically or mentally, was blessed, not by a conscious direction of his mind, because that would have been trying to use God and send it over to some person. No, he was living in the contemplation of divine grace, and then let anybody, saint or sinner, touch him, and instantly be purified.

This is an example of the unconditioned mind resting within itself, the abiding place of the spirit, not functioning with concepts, beliefs, or theories, but dwelling "in the secret place of the most High,"[21] tabernacling with Him within, taking no thought. The whole world is overcome in that abiding. His grace is our sufficiency without trying to take thought for His grace. His grace is our sufficiency. His presence is fulfillment unto our experience. Outwardly it may appear as success in some endeavor, but all of that is the appearance.

We let this mind be in us "which was also in Christ Jesus," but we do not let thoughts of this world intrude into our mind, not even thoughts of improving this world. We let the mind that was in Christ Jesus be in us, and It will function. It will give us the new melodies we may be looking for, the new ideas, the new principles, the new discoveries, or the new inventions. It will provide shelters, high towers, hiding places in Him. Only we must take no thought for the things of this world, and let the Christ within us give us light. While we are taking no thought, this presence of God within us will speak, will reveal and empower us.

Being Endowed From on High

In the new English Bible there is a passage where Jesus is making his farewell to his disciples before departing from the world: "So stay here in this city until you are armed with the power from above."[22] That is exactly our attitude in meditation. We abide in the meditation until we are empowered from on high, until we have received His grace, His strength, His wisdom, His law. We do not believe that our affirmations of truth are going to be the light of God, the wisdom, or the strength of God. They are not! Those affirmations, silently declared within us, may bring us to a place of silence where we receive His grace, where we receive power from on high. Then as we go out into the world we will find that His power goes with us, His wisdom,

His strength, His love. We can understand why the Master could say, "Why callest thou me good?"[23] When we retire within, we are endowed from on high, we are empowered with love from on high. It is not our love: it is His love. We are merely the instruments through which it is flowing.

When we go into meditation, we want to "stay here in this city until we are armed with the power from above," until we actually feel that the spirit of God indwells us, that His robe is upon us, His grace, is with us, for His grace is our sufficiency. Only remember, let there be no conditioned thinking about this world. We leave this world and its problems, its wants, its limitations, its desires outside when we go into communion, and we do not try to think that we are going to bring this inner communion into the outer world. It will not work. We keep this communion within ourselves until we feel empowered from above, and then we go about our business and find that It literally goes before us to straighten out all the rough places. It really goes before us to provide and to multiply the loaves and fishes if necessary.

Abiding in Our Withinness
Translates Itself Into Harmony Without

The barrier to success is trying to connect spirit with this world. When we go into meditation, we leave this world out. Then we have overcome the world and are abiding in "the secret place of the most High," and there receive spiritual illumination. That is all we want: spiritual illumination within, and no connecting it with any outer circumstance or condition.

> "I have overcome the world."
> I am not taking the world into my meditation:
> it is outside. I am inside in the kingdom of God
> within me. I and the Father tabernacle together.
> I commune with the Father within me.

I recognize His presence and His grace.
I recognize His love, His peace, and His joy,
and all of this within me.

There is not a single thought in my mind of any world outside my own being, and yet I am convinced of this, because I
have witnessed it, that this tabernacling within produces har-
monies in the experience of students out here. All that takes
place in the withinness translates itself into terms of harmony in
the experience of those who touch us, not because of any do-
gooder complex, not because of trying to use God for some person, but because of a willingness to leave the world outside.

This is a spiritual kingdom within us. This is a spiritual universe, and there are spiritual people in "My kingdom," spiritual
children of God, and we are all heirs of God, joint-heirs to all the
heavenly riches. The branch on the right side of the tree is fed
from the same source as is the branch on the left side of the tree.

"I have overcome the world."
I am home in Thee. I am fed from an inner source.
The Christ gives me my cup of water,
and this cup of water springs up into wellsprings of
life eternal. I am fed from within,
clothed from within, housed from within.

The kingdom of God is within me, and it is a spiritual feeding, a spiritual drinking, a spiritual housing, a
temple of God, not made with hands.

The Activity of the Christ Dispels the Illusion

This is not a physical universe, nor are we turning to spirit
to do something to a physical universe. We have overcome the
physical universe, and we are wholly and completely at-one in
spirit, all of us together in a oneness of spiritual communion:

one household of God, one family, one fountain of God, in His house of many mansions.

As we return to the problems of human existence, they are no longer our problems. In fact, they are no longer problems. Now we see them as shadows without substance, without power, and we can look on them, regardless of their name or nature—whether "man whose breath is in his nostrils"[24] or a hurricane—and see them as shadows, having no power because we have already felt that all-power within us. There is no power left to be in the hurricane, no power left in the whirlwind, no power left to be in "man, whose breath is in his nostrils," for all-power is within us.

Then we walk up and down this world and see it, almost as the shadows on a moving picture screen, knowing that they come and they go, but they have no real substance, no real voice, no real power. In this way we bring the activity of the Christ to human consciousness and dispel the illusion of two powers. We dispel the illusion of good men and bad men, because now there are no bad men and no good men: there is only God, all good.

In meditation, the Christ is to be kept in the kingdom of God within us, so that when we return to the world, it can be the light that shows us that everything out here is shadow.

TAPE RECORDED EXCERPTS
Prepared by the Editor

When mind is a pure instrument, it is unconditioned by the belief of good or evil in form or effect. It is then a clear transparency, revealing the divine perfection that has always existed, exists now, and always will exist. The following excerpts will help to gain a better understanding of this subject:

The Unconditioned Mind

"I do not have to get rid of the mind; I do not have to overcome mortal mind; I do not have to destroy it: I have to understand that my mind is an instrument for my soul, and it becomes that by filling my mind with spiritual truth and grace. My mind imbued with truth is the law of resurrection, renewal, regeneration, restoration. . . .

"At first it works this way: you fill your mind with spiritual truth, not with the truth that is going to overcome something or do something. Fill it with truth: 'I and my Father are one.' . . . God's grace is my sufficiency. . . . Where the spirit of the Lord is, there is freedom.

"Living in that atmosphere, feeding consciousness with these truths for a certain length of time—and the time differs with each one—there comes a specific day, a specific moment, when that truth takes over the mind, and no longer does the mind have to be filled with truth, but truth acts to keep the mind continuously in tune with the infinite. From then on, the flow is the other way. It is not you thinking truth, remembering truth, declaring truth, and meditating on truth: it is truth using your consciousness for its expression. You almost become like a vacuum, listening, and it always is using you. It is flowing through you."

Joel S. Goldsmith, "The Infinite Way: Origin and Principle,"
The First 1957 Halekou Closed Class.

"There is only one mind, and it is unconditioned. It is neither good nor bad; it has no qualities of good or of evil. It is an
unconditioned mind, a state of being, not good and not bad. .
. . There cannot be intelligent mind and ignorant mind; there
cannot be healthy mind and diseased mind, for mind is unconditioned.

"Mind as body is unconditioned, and therefore, body is neither well nor sick, tall nor short, thin nor fat. Body is as unconditioned as the mind which is the essence of its form. . . . When
you understand the nature of mind appearing as form, mind
unconditioned by good or evil, you will then have a body which
is neither good nor evil."

Joel S. Goldsmith, "Unconditioned Mind and Life,"
The 1959 Manchester Closed Class.

Chapter Twelve

Spiritual Preparation
for Peace

Many students, even after they are on the spiritual path, think that there is some truth or some message to be found in a book or in the Bible that will change the nature of their life, that is, improve it, and do it quickly. The truth is that there is no message or teaching that can have that much power.

Truth Cannot Be Revealed
Through the Mind

There is a truth, however, a startling truth, revealed by the great mystics of all ages, but it cannot be accepted by most persons because it cannot be understood through the mind. "The natural man receiveth not the things of the Spirit of God."[1] Therefore, the natural man, with this reasoning, thinking mind, can never grasp truth, and even if by some miracle the truth could be given to that mind it would benefit no one.

There is a story that goes back probably five thousand years illustrating this, relating to a time when the ultimate of truth was known, and some who wanted to know this truth were determined to find it. It has always been believed that it would take a person anywhere from six to nine years to be able to grasp

202 The Journey Back to the Father's House

truth, even though when the truth was given to him it could be given to him in one sentence. It has always been considered, even four or five thousand years ago, that there must be a period of from six to nine years before an individual's consciousness could be prepared to receive the truth. These men, however, were determined to have it sooner than that and to bypass those years of inner preparation. But whether or not they received it, it did them no good.

Ever since that time, men have tried to give forth truth in a capsule or even in a book, but it is not possible. The mind of the natural man, the mind with which or into which he is born, cannot accept truth. Because of that, there must be a period between the time that a person's interest in truth is aroused and the time when his consciousness is prepared to accept it, that is, when he arrives at a point of spiritual discernment. Paul made this clear in his teachings when he spoke of the inability of "the natural man" to receive truth. Even though the ultimate statement of truth were given to us, it would be meaningless.

Spiritual Discernment
Brings Realization Closer

For many years we have had a Christmas message each December. They are all preserved in our books of the Letters that have been published, and if you read these messages, you will find that, although the principles do not vary, a different idea is brought to light in each message. Furthermore, if you were to read all of these Christmas messages, at the end of the reading you would discover that you would have a fuller grasp of the nature of Christmas than simply by reading one of them.

In other words, a little something or other would come back from each of these past messages to form a greater whole. Actually, what has happened is that your own consciousness has developed over the years so that what you heretofore had read only with the mind you now are beginning to discern through the soul faculties, through the power of spiritual discernment. You are getting closer and closer to the point of realization.

In the Presence of a Developed Spiritual Consciousness, Evil Is Not Power

Over and over, you have heard it said that error is not power, that evil is not power, disease is not power, and even sin is not power. This is a very satisfying philosophy, and everyone would like to believe it. In fact, I don't know of anything that could be more pleasant and comforting to believe than that disease is not power, that sin is not power, or that lack, limitation, and poverty are not power. But you are faced with a world in which, not only is evil power, but it seems to be a great deal more powerful than good.

Yet, Christ Jesus taught and demonstrated that *in the presence of spiritual consciousness, the fourth dimensional consciousness,* the evils of this world are not power. He not only taught this, he demonstrated it in the healing of sin, disease, and lack. He proved conclusively that wherever he walked, the nothingness, the nonpower, of human evil was demonstrated. He also proved that wherever his disciples walked, evil had less power, not to the extent that it was nullified as it was in his presence because, as he indicated, the disciples had not yet attained a sufficient fullness of the spiritual or fourth dimensional consciousness. Therefore, what metaphysics has really been saying, or should have been saying, is that in the presence of either a natural or a cultivated spiritual consciousness, evil loses its power, and the spiritual power of good is revealed.

It has been proved in the past century that evil loses its reality and its power wherever there is an individual who either has come into this world with a fourth dimensional consciousness, or wherever, through study, application, and devotion, this consciousness has been developed. While there is no longer any question that this is true, it was a question when it was originally brought to the attention of the world.

Increasing Interest in Spiritual Healing

For years, the idea of spiritual healing was bitterly fought by the church and by *materia medica,* even to the point of challenging its practice in the courts. Today, however, not only is spiritual healing not fought but, as a matter of fact, such teachings are encouraged in many places. It was quite a concession for a newspaper, just outside of Washington, D.C., to print an editorial a few years ago in which the writer acknowledged that spiritual healing has been proved and is here to stay. The editor who wrote the editorial had not been aware of the possibility of spiritual healing before and was surprised because he had heard about it only recently.

When you hear that more and more churches are encouraging the study and practice of spiritual healing and that in some areas in the medical world, physicians, too, are investigating this subject, what you, as a pioneer, will have to keep in mind is that the only contribution you can make is in the degree that you, yourself, know that there is nothing of a miraculous nature about spiritual healing. It is not the bringing of God into the picture in order to get God to do what a doctor cannot do or what a minister cannot do. I believe that this has been a deterrent to a widespread understanding of spiritual healing. Too many people have believed that God is doing for them what heretofore they expected their minister or their doctor to do. And this really has held back the understanding of the entire subject.

Christmas Antedates the Birth of Jesus

Christmas is involved in this entire subject of healing because, in the religious world, Christmas has been identified

with the birth of a man known far and wide for his great healing gift. Actually, the birth of a man has nothing whatsoever to
do with Christmas. Christmas has to do with the birth of the
Christ, the birth, recognition, or the coming to awareness of the
transcendental consciousness, which before the birth of the
Christ in consciousness is not only unknown, but cannot be
experienced.

For example, Moses was a shepherd, in spite of the fact that
he had been highly educated in Egypt, not only educated in all
the culture, science, and wisdom of that age, but also in the
occult. A transformation took place in Moses on a Christmas
Day, a day in which was born in the consciousness of Moses the
realization of the truth of this transcendental spiritual consciousness, that which is above knowing or being known, that
which is above the mind, that which really comes only in a period of unknowing, in a period of silence, when the mind, with
its reasoning and thinking faculties, is still. Then it becomes
possible to receive from the infinite consciousness an awareness
of that infinite consciousness.

We are born only into a knowledge of our own limited
human mentality. Except for the few who are blessed with coming into this world mystically, we have no awareness in our early
experience that there is anything beyond our mind. We have no
knowledge that there is anything beyond whatever wisdom we
are able to pick up between the cradle and the grave. But, to
Moses, in this instant of high consciousness or awareness, there
came the experience. In mystical literature this is sometimes
called "the Presence." In the Oriental world it is called "the
Buddha-mind," or "Satori," a moment of illumination.

Whatever name you give it, what really happens is that an
ordinary human being, with no knowledge other than what
his own human mentality provided, in an instant becomes
aware of something greater than himself, something greater
than his mind, something greater than his knowledge. In fact,
from this Christmas moment, that is, from the moment of the

divine birth, a knowledge and wisdom pour into the individual that is far greater than anyone has ever had solely from the reading of books.

In teaching this, the Master said, "Before Abraham was, I am."[2] This transcendental Self, this divine consciousness, existed before the birth of Jesus. In fact, It existed before Abraham. The reason Jesus referred to Abraham, who had the conviction of one God, was that Abraham was looked upon as the father of the Hebrews, the one who departed from the pagan worship of many gods to the worship of one God. With that came the beginning of Judaism. Before there was a Hebrew religion, however, this divine consciousness existed, and It existed and manifested Itself as the experience of Abraham, Moses, and Jesus. But It existed before Abraham, Moses, and Jesus.

Jesus Revealed That Christ Consciousness Is Available to All

The significance of Christmas is not that Jesus was born, but that the Christ was revealed. The importance of Christmas now, is not that the birth of a man should be celebrated, though this would not detract in any way from your love of, or respect for the man, or your appreciation of the man's devotion, but rather that you understand why you have this feeling of veneration and love for Jesus Christ. He was one of the few who had the courage to reveal to the world that this is not the secret about a holy man, but this is the secret of a holy consciousness which was before Abraham, and which is available to all mankind, to all who will open themselves to the Christ.

As you read and hear the Christmas story year in and year out, eventually it goes beyond your mind and reaches that part of you which can be awakened. Every child who is born has an area of his consciousness which is dormant, and insofar as mankind is concerned, most men and women go through their entire lifetime without this area of consciousness ever being awakened. It is only the few in the history of the world who have ever had the experience of the awakening of that dormant part of consciousness.

For centuries, it was believed that this could happen only to the few. In ancient Egypt and until approximately 200 A.D., it was known that those who had an inclination toward the spiritual life and who could find a teacher on the spiritual path could be awakened. After that, in the Western World, this possibility was omitted from most teachings and, therefore, the only record there is of any persons who have been awakened are those who came to it through some inner experience of their own without being able to account for it.

Opening Consciousness

One well-known illustration of spiritual awakening through an inner experience is found in the life of Jacob Boehme, the German cobbler, who, for some unknown reason, while actually cobbling in his shop, looked up and saw the sun shining on a rock. Something happened within himself, between him and that ray of sunshine on the rock, and suddenly his inner consciousness was opened, and he discerned spiritually; he saw reality. he became the father of modern mysticism, and had many followers who were opened through him or through his teaching.

In the Orient, particularly in India and Japan, the teaching never died out that if you could find a spiritually enlightened individual, one in whom this soul-center was open, that individual could open the student's. And so we have had spiritual students in the Orient all through the ages.

You may wonder why the consciousness of every student who went to these men was not opened. The answer lies in the word *dedication.* Many would like to have their consciousness opened; many would like to be spiritually illumined if only it could be done in their spare time and with spare change. If only it will not take too much time or too much money is the hue and cry deep down within most persons who set out on the path. When you let the element of time and money enter, you soon find antagonism to the spiritual awakening.

Just what part does time play? If this were merely an intellectual truth which could be imparted, then it would be necessary only to own a Hebrew Testament, a Christian Testament, or Oriental Scripture, and it would be done. There is sufficient truth in any of these to do it. Furthermore, there have been some very good metaphysical and mystical writers of this past century, and in any of the authentic ones there is enough truth to bring about the opening of consciousness. But it is not the truth that will do it: it is knowing the truth, and that knowing does not mean reading it, affirming it, or stating it. It really means knowing it, that is, attaining the actual awareness of it. And that takes time. You can read these books and, as I have told our students so often in class instruction, if you think for a moment that the truth lies in my books, you are going to look in vain, because you can read them all the way through and not find it.

The truth is within your consciousness. The reading of these books, the study of them, and the practice of the principles will lead you to that truth within yourself, which you develop, and in the end bring about the Christ-birth. The books will not do it of themselves. Your dedication is what will do it.

Where does money enter into all of this? Books cost money; teachers must live; centers must be provided or paid for. It is not that the money in and of itself will buy it for anyone. There is no use for anyone to believe that he can write out a check for a thousand or ten thousand dollars and have it. No, it is not money in that sense. You cannot buy it with money. Nevertheless, there is a certain amount of money involved in the incidentals.

What Is Security?

How does one attain this Christ-awareness and hold it close within? A book, published for children, a tiny little one by a cartoonist, with the title *Security,* is a delightful and entertaining piece about what security is. It gives a number of examples of what security means to different persons. It shows a dog and his dog house, and it says that security is when you own your own home. There is a schoolboy coming home from school, and it explains that security is when you find your mother at home in the kitchen when you get there. Security is having someone to lean on. It is a little book of cartoons, showing the different ways in which security is made evident to children and animals.

But what is security from the Infinite Way standpoint? Security lies in meditation; security lies in grace; security lies in the withinness; security lies in understanding the nature of God and individual consciousness. There you have the essence of it. When an Infinite Way student believes that truth is in a book, in a teaching, in a church, or in a teacher, he is making it external, just as much outside of himself as if he placed his security in his property, in his employment, or in someone to lean upon.

Spiritual truth and wisdom are not found in a book. You may search the scriptures thinking that you will find truth therein. No, the scriptures reveal where truth is to be found. And where is that? Within you. Even books of mysticism and spiritual wisdom cannot give you truth: they can only reveal where truth is to be found. They can also reveal where health, safety, and security are to be found.

The individual student must locate it there within himself and there experience it, so that, like Moses, Isaiah, and Jesus, he actually has the experience of the birth of the Christ, the awakening of that transcendental consciousness which reveals to him, "Be not afraid, *I* am with you." Then, with a start of surprise he realizes what Moses said, *"I Am That I Am."*[3] That is what Isaiah said: *I, I.* That is what Jesus revealed: "I am the bread of life."[4] Man shall not live by bread alone, for *I* am the substance, the food, *I,* this spirit of God within me, which is that *I* that existed before Abraham, not Jesus who was born two thousand years ago but *I,* who am before Abraham, *I* am the substance of your life, the law of health, of purity.

Your Christmas Day, a Day of Renewed Dedication

You must learn the nature of God and prayer, even if only intellectually at first. Abide with that intellectual understanding, live with it, practice it, until you, too have your Christmas morning, a morning of spiritual rebirth, a dawning in your consciousness of the nature of the Christ.

When the Christ is born in you, evil begins to lose its reality. Do not expect that it is all going to disappear in one breaking of a bubble, because it is not that way. It is not that way in individual experience, not in the experience of most students. It is an abiding with this Christmas-experience, making every day of the year a Christmas Day, a day of new birth, new dedication, and letting this Christ-spirit that dawns on a specific date increase. Let *It* become more and more powerful until eventually It takes over.

Christmas Day for Paul was the day in which he said, "I live; yet not I, but Christ liveth in me."[5] It was not the man Jesus that lived his life; that man had been crucified. It was the Christ who took over the life of Paul and lived his life, went before him to "make the crooked places straight,"[6] spoke through his lips, financed the churches when the churches could not finance themselves.

Your First Christmas Does Not Mean There Will Be No More Problems

So it is that with the first spiritual awakening, you begin to perceive that error lessens in your experience, probably slowly. Sometimes there is a healing of one nature or another that appears to be a miracle and is, to your sense. Do not be fooled by this and believe that all of a sudden you have the miracle of life, the key to life, and that your entire experience is going to be of that nature, because it is not true.

Even as Paul was teaching and preaching the Christ, he had to take a few bad licks from the human mind. Even the Master, Christ Jesus, who contributed so much to our knowledge of this transcendental consciousness, even he had to pay the price of crucifixion. Therefore, do not believe that this really means that with the birth of your first Christ-experience, your first Christmas, you will live the rest of your days without problems, because it does not work that way.

There may be quite a few periods of illness or lack until you, yourself, are deeply rooted in the Christ and this Christ completely takes over your experience. Then, of course, there will be the experience of others who come to you for healing and then for teaching, and vicariously you will experience the suffering in their lives and their problems, and it will be just as hard for you as if you, yourself, were undergoing the problem, and sometimes worse. Many a time you will have the feeling that you would rather take this problem over and suffer for a person than see the person suffering, but you will not be able to do this because life is an individual experience.

The birth of the Christ is your Christmas Day and mine. It is that particular moment in which there is something in the nature of an awakening or in the nature of an awareness in which you realize that something is now functioning of which you heretofore were unaware. It may only be in fleeting glimpses. It may be in a few individual experiences, but for all, the experience is the same.

Spiritual Maturity

Paul had to wait nine years for the fulfillment of the Christ in him before he could go out into the ministry. I was thrown into the healing ministry within two years after my first experience, but I was not given the teaching ministry for sixteen more years. It is very slow in developing, very slow maturing. The reason is found in the understanding of the word *maturity.*

Maturity is the ability to think objectively, not through the conditioned mind. A person may be forty, fifty, sixty, or seventy years of age and still be immature. A person may have PhDs in several fields of knowledge and be immature, because maturity has nothing to do with age or education. Maturity has to do only with the ability to think objectively, to see understandingly, to throw off the conditioning that has come about through birth, race, or education.

Every time a person who has been brought up in some orthodox religion is able to throw off the restrictions of a belief in a personalized God, and can realize that God never was a Hebrew, a Christian, or a Buddhist, but that God is spirit, he has attained his maturity.

Those, who, regardless of their education or age, must still personalize God, are immature. Maturity is not given to a person, however, except by an inner grace. There is a *something* within him that prepares him for maturity. When maturity comes, it brings with it a spiritual maturity, the dawning of this something of which he had not previously been aware. This something actually goes before him to "make the crooked places straight," to prepare "mansions"[7] for him where heretofore there were hovels or ghettos.

Christ-Consciousness Ensures Freedom

The freedom that the Christian can know in an atheistic world, the Hebrew is to know in a Christian world, the freedom that the black man is to know in a white world, the freedom that an Oriental is to know in a Western World, this freedom is not going to be attained by armies or by protest marches. This freedom is going to be attained through education, culture, and then spiritual development. These are the three steps necessary for the attainment of individual and collective freedom.

You must never forget that in this land of the stars and stripes we have witnessed the lack of freedom many minorities have suffered. In New England, both the Jew and the Roman Catholic have experienced it. In the South in the past, the Negro and the Jew have experienced it, and the Catholic. In most parts of our nation, the Oriental has experienced it. But to all these the answer is the same. They have to earn their freedom, not through force but through education, through culture, through spiritual development until they are recognized by their fellow men as equal, until every person is recognized by every other one as an equal, not because there is an army in back of him, but because the way in which he or she lives his or her life testifies to equality.

Loosing the Christ
Into Human Consciousness

In the 1960's the United States was faced with more and more marches trying to enforce freedom, setting American against American. The only solution will be if we, as pioneers on the mystical path, can receive the Christ and loose the Christ, so that the evil and error in human consciousness loses its power in the presence of the Christ, which those on the spiritual path have loosed into the world.

It lies within your power to accept this truth that there is in the consciousness of every individual the Christ, the son of God, the spirit of God. This presence exists in the consciousness of every individual on the face of the globe, and the spiritually illumined can awaken It in those still unillumined, those unable to recognize the Christ within.

As an illustration let us suppose that you are my student and I am your teacher. What is my method of awakening you to spiritual awareness? First, I meditate. I meditate in order to bring myself to the realization that within me is the kingdom of

God, the Christ, the spirit of God, the son of God, or the presence and power of God so that I and my Father are consciously one. If this is true of me, I would have to be a horrible egotist not to realize that this is by divine decree. In other words, it is the decree of God that this son of God be established in me. So I must realize God can have no special children. This same presence is within you. God in the midst of you is mighty, the spirit of God within you.

So, as I meditate on this, I realize in every one of you that Christ sits enthroned. The very spirit of God which is your bread is the source of your wisdom because God is the mind of you. You cannot love of yourself. Love is of God; therefore, the love in your heart is really the love of God enthroned there. Thus the wisdom of God is enthroned in your mind, and the love of God is enthroned in you. With that recognition, I become still—no more thoughts, no more words, as I let the peace of God descend upon me. I let His spirit bear witness with my spirit that this is truth.

I remain for as long as I can in inner stillness, inner quietness—no thoughts, no words—that the spirit of God Itself may bear witness with my spirit and yours. Sooner or later, whether it happens the first time or the hundredth and first time, I feel an answering response within me, a weight dropping off my shoulders, an inner peace, and then I know that His spirit has registered.

It may not register in every one of you on every occasion, but I am sure that one of you, or two or three of you, will have responded and felt this presence touch you. So it is that in time, It reaches every one of you to some extent, and then you, yourself, must carry on from there to bring It into Its fullness.

Each time that you meditate, every day of the week that you meditate for this purpose, someone out in the world is being awakened. It could be a president; it could be a senator; it could be a congressman; it could be a prime minister; it could be someone somewhere. It could be a minister, a priest, a rabbi:

you do not know and you do not care. You are not here to get credit and you are not here to be praised. You are here for only one reason. You do know that everyone who receives some measure of spiritual illumination can awaken in some measure those who are still asleep. Therefore, this is your function, and this is your contribution to the peace of the nation and to the peace of the world.

Realize within yourself the Christ, the Christmas Day. Let every day be a Christmas Day of realization, and then loose that Christ into the world and let It touch those who are prepared.

TAPE RECORDED EXCERPTS
Prepared by the Editor

The *Letter* this month points up how important it is for serious students to review the Christmas messages found in the published writings of Joel S. Goldsmith, all of which make clear that those moments of illumination mark the birth of the Christ in individual consciousness. These lessons were given to students in regular class sessions, held at various times of the year, again proving that Christmas can be any or every day of the year. The Christmas messages are listed below, together with the particular tape recorded classes from which these chapters in the writings were taken.

Christmas

"Christmas 1955," Chapter 12 of *The 1955 Infinite Way Letters* from Joel S. Goldsmith's "The Christ on Earth," *The 1955 First Kailua Study Group.*

"Tithing with Melchizedek," Chapter 12 of *The 1957 Infinite Way Letters* from Joel S. Goldsmith's "Melchizedek, The Babe, Act of Devotion," *The 1955 First Kailua Study Group.*

"The One Great Miracle," Chapter 12 in *The 1958 Infinite Way Letters* from Joel S. Goldsmith's "The Christ," *The First 1956 Steinway Hall Closed Class.*

"Christhood," Chapter 12, in *The 1959 Infinite Way Letters* from "Christhood," *The Second 1953 New York Practitioners' Class.*

"The Principle of Nonpower," Chapter 12 in *Our Spiritual Resources*, from Joel S. Goldsmith's "The Principle of No Power," *The 1959 Maui Advanced Work.*

"The Spiritual Christmas," Chapter 12 in *The Contemplative Life* from Joel S. Goldsmith's "The Spiritual Christmas (Christmas Day 1960)," *The 1960-61 Christmas and New Year's, Waikiki.*

"The Prince of Peace," Chapter 12 in *Man Was Not Born to Cry* from Joel S. Goldsmith's "The Principle of Power and Love," *The 1962 Princess Kaiulani Open Class.*

"God Revealing Himself as Christ on Earth," Chapter 12 in *Beyond Words and Thoughts* from Joel S. Goldsmith's "God Revealing Himself as Christ on Earth," *The 1963 Kailua Private Class,* and "Summarizing the New Message," *The 1963 Kailua Private Class.*

"Christ is the Consciousness of Mankind," Chapter 12 in *Consciousness Is What I Am* from Joel S. Goldsmith's "Christ as the Consciousness of Mankind," *The 1963 Los Angeles Special Class,* and "The New Message 1963 (to Teachers, Practitioners, and Group Leaders)," *The 1963 London Work.*

You will also be interested in the following excerpts from the recordings on the meaning of Christmas:

"The Christ is a state of being, a state of consciousness, a state of awareness, a presence, a power, a something very tangible. There is no mistaking the Christ when you see It. . . . The Christ Itself is without form and yet It appears very much as form.

"The innate spiritual Christ, which is the true center of everyone's being, can be drawn forth. . . with time, with patience, with love. It cannot come forth before Its time, any more than a child can be born before its time. . . . The Christ can only come into truth in Its time, and that time is the time of your unfolding consciousness. That is why there are those who catch the realization and the vision of the Christ instantly. Whether they had a preparation on this plane or the one before, we do not know, but some catch it very quickly. . . . With others, it is a long drawn out process. . . . That we do not attain It in this year or on this plane or on the next plane is of no great moment. Those who have turned to the Word will find It revealed. . . . This is an era when this unveiled Christ will appear in human consciousness. We are instruments of It.

"There is nothing personal about the Christ except that the Christ appears personally as your consciousness and mine. It is personal in the sense that we receive It. It is personal to us just as It was personal to Jesus and to those of his disciples who received It. So It is personal to us, but It is not personal in the sense that It is something that you or I can claim as of, or for, our own selves. . . . This is the spirit of God in individual consciousness, and It must come to those who are prepared for It. . . . There is only one way in which the Christ can come to earth this time, and that is as It is received in individual consciousness."

Joel S. Goldsmith, "Isaiah's Prophecy of the Christ,"
The 1953 New York Practitioners' Class.

"There is no Christ-experience for anyone while he is living on the human plane. There must be a purification of consciousness, which is called a baptism of the spirit, a descent of the Holy Ghost, in which you lose human judgment, criticism, condemnation, in which you are of too pure eyes to behold iniquity. . . . That is, then, the state of consciousness that can receive the Christ because that is the pure, or virgin, state of consciousness. It does not have two powers. It does not believe in the pain of the flesh, but neither does it believe in the pleasures of the flesh. It has neither pain nor pleasure: it has only God, only spiritual enlightenment and spiritual joy and spiritual health. . . . It is a completely virgin state of consciousness. . . . When you are not a house divided against yourself, when you are not a consciousness divided against yourself, you are pure, and the Christ can find entrance and the Christ has a name. It always comes to you with the name *I*."

Joel S. Goldsmith, "The Virgin Consciousness,"
The 1960 Melbourne Closed Class.

Jan 10, 2016 1st reading

About the Series

The 1971 through 1981 *Letters* will be published as a series of eleven fine-quality soft cover books. Each book published in the first edition will be offered by Acropolis Books and The Valor Foundation, and can be ordered from either source:

ACROPOLIS BOOKS, INC.
8601 Dunwoody Place
Suite 303
Atlanta, GA 30350-2509
(800) 773-9923
acropolisbooks@mindspring.com

THE VALOR FOUNDATION
1101 Hillcrest Drive
Hollywood, FL 33021
(954) 989-3000
info@valorfoundation.com

Scriptural References and Notes

CHAPTER ONE:

1. Psalm 91:1.
2. Matthew 11:11.
3. Romans 8:17.
4. Luke 17:20,21.
5. Hebrews 4:12.
6. John 17:3.
7. John 5:30.
8. John 14:10.
9. Psalm 139:8.
10. Psalm 23:4.
11. John 14:4.
12. Psalm 91:1.
13. I Samuel 3:9.
14. I Kings 19:12.
15. Luke 15:31.
16. Isaiah 45:2.
17. Matthew 18:22.
18. Luke 23:34.
19. Matthew 5:38.
20. John 8:11.
21. Luke 23:43.
22. Ezekiel 18:32.
23. John 19:11.
24. II Chronicles 32:8.
25. Isaiah 2:22.
26. Romans 8:38,39.

CHAPTER TWO:

1. Mark 10:15.
2. Matthew 5:45.
3. John 15:13.
4. John 19:11.
5. John 5:8.
6. Matthew 14:19.
7. John 8:11.
8. Luke 17:21.
9. Exodus 3:5.
10. Psalm 16:11.
11. Proverbs 3:5,6.
12. Deuteronomy 6:5.
13. II Corinthians 12:9.
14. II Chronicles 32:8.
15. Psalm 23:4.
16. Romans 8:38,39.
17. By the author.
   (Acropolis Books,
   Atlanta, GA. 1999)
18. Psalm 139:12.
19. Romans 3:4.
20. John 12:45.

CHAPTER THREE

1. Philippians 2:5.
2. John 7:24.
3. John 8:11.
4. Luke 12:14.
5. John 11:25.
6. John 6:35.
7. Matthew 4:4.
8. John 4:32.
9. John 4:34.
10. Luke 17:21.
11. Exodus 3:5.
12. Psalm 146:3.
13. Hebrews 13:6.
14. Matthew 26:52.
15. Psalm 91:1,10.
16. Isaiah 2:22.
17. Luke 15:31.
18. Romans 8:38,39.
19. Luke 23:34.
20. By the author.
    (Harper Collins,
    New York. 1993)
21. By the author.
    (Acropolis Books,
    Atlanta, GA. 1997)
22. By the author.
    (Harper Collins,
    New York. 1990)
23. Isaiah 45:2.
24. John 14:2.
25. By the author.
    (Acropolis Books,
    Atlanta, GA. 1997)

26. John 8:32.
27. Matthew 23:37.
28. Matthew 25:40,45.

CHAPTER FOUR

1. Matthew 9:17.
2. John 18:36.
3. John 14:27.
4. Matthew 6:25.
5. Matthew 6:27.
6. Matthew 6:33.
7. Luke 17:21.
8. I Kings 19:12.
9. Psalm 46:6.
10. Robert Browning.
11. I Samuel 3:9.
12. Psalm 46:10.
13. Isaiah 45:2.
14. Matthew 3:17.
15. Luke 15:31.
16. Hebrews 13:5.
17. Matthew 23:9.
18. I Corinthians 3:16.
19. I Corinthians 6:19.
20. John 10:30.
21. Matthew 25:40,45.
22. John 15:7.

CHAPTER FIVE

1. Matthew 6:33.
2. John 4:24.
3. Romans 8:26.
4. John 10:30.
5. Isaiah 61:1.
6. Galatians 2:20.
7. Alfred, Lord Tennyson.
8. Matthew 6:13.
9. John 14:10.
10. I Samuel 3:9.
11. Luke 15:31.
12. John 8:32.
13. Matthew 13:46.
14. Hebrews 13:5.
15. Psalm 19:1.
16. John 5:30.
17. I Kings 19:12.

CHAPTER SIX

1. I Kings 17:11.
2. I Kings 17:12.
3. I Kings 17:16.
4. Mark 6:38.
5. Mark 6:41.
6. John 17:3.
7. Exodus 33:14.
8. Isaiah 45:2.
9. John 8:32.
10. Proverbs 3:5.
11. Exodus 3:5.
12. Job 23:14.
13. Hebrews 13:5.
14. Genesis 26:24.
15. Matthew 5:46.
16. Matthew 5:44.
17. John 5:30.
18. John 14:10.
19. Matthew 4:4.
20. John 16:7.
21. Matthew 3:15.
22. Matthew 10:8.
23. Matthew 10:7.
24. John 4:8.
25. Psalm 46:10.
26. John 14:2.
27. Romans 8:38,39.
28. II Corinthians 12:9.
29. Luke 17:21.
30. Job 32:8.

CHAPTER SEVEN

1. Matthew 23:9.
2. Matthew 25:40.
3. John 10:30.
4. By the author, *The Infinite Way*
5. By the author, *Practicing the Presence*
6. By the author. (Acropolis Books, Atlanta, GA. 1997)
7. John 8:32.
8. Matthew 25:45.
9. Acts 10:34.
10. I John 4:20.
11. John 4:32.
12. Exodus 3:14.
13. John 12:45.
14. John 10:10.

CHAPTER EIGHT

1. John 4:32.
2. John 10:30.
3. Matthew 6:10.
4. Matthew 7:20.
5. II Chronicles 32:8.
6. John 7:24.
7. John 18:38.
8. Luke 4:8.
9. Matthew 3:10.
10. Romans 8:7.
11. John 4:32.

CHAPTER NINE

1. I Kings 19:12.
2. Psalm 46:6.
3. Genesis 18:32.
4. John 4:22.
5. I Corinthians 13:12.
6. Matthew 26:52.
7. Matthew 5:39.
8. Matthew 12:25.
9. Mark 8:18.
10. Hebrews 13:5.
11. Matthew 28:20.
12. Isaiah 2:22.
13. Ephesians 5:14.
14. John 14:27.
15. John 18:36.
16. Luke 15:31.
17. John 10:30.
18. John 15:5.
19. Galatians 2:20.
20. Philippians 4:13.
21. Acts 10:34.
22. John 15:6.

CHAPTER TEN

1. Exodus 20:5.
2. Proverbs 23:7.
3. Exodus 20:4.
4. John 9:25.
5. Isaiah 2:22.
6. Psalm 23:4.
7. Exodus 3:5.
8. Matthew 22:37-40.
9. John 5:30.
10. Matthew 10:8.
11. Galatians 6:7,8.
12. Psalm 146:3.
13. Isaiah 2:22.
14. John 10:10.
15. Luke 12:25.
16. Matthew 6:12.
17. I Corinthians 15:26.
18. Luke 15:31.

CHAPTER ELEVEN

1. Philippians 2:5.
2. Luke 17:21.
3. John 6:45.
4. Robert Browning.
5. Luke 15:31.
6. Robert Browning.
7. I Samuel 3:9.
8. Galatians 2:20.
9. Isaiah 45:2.
10. Psalm 46:6.
11. I Kings 19:12.
12. John 16:33.

13. John 18:36.
14. John 14:27.
15. Philippians 4:7.
16. I Kings 17:6.
17. I Kings 17:10.
18. I Corinthians 3:16.
19. Romans 8:14,16,17.
20. II Corinthians 12:9.
21. Psalm 91:1.
22. Luke 24:49,
    New English Bible.
23. Matthew 19:17.
24. Isaiah 2:22.

CHAPTER TWELVE

1. Corinthians 2:14.
2. John 8:58.
3. Exodus 3:14.
4. John 6:35.
5. Galatians 2:20.
6. Isaiah 45:2.
7. John 14:2.

Joel Goldsmith
Tape Recorded Classes
Corresponding to the
Chapters of this Volume

Tape recordings may be ordered from

THE INFINITE WAY
PO Box 2089, Peoria AZ 85380-2089
Telephone 800-922-3195 Fax 623-412-8766

E-mail: infiniteway@earthlink.net
www.joelgoldsmith.com
Free Catalog Upon Request

Chapter 1:   Meditation: Its Function and Purpose
             #424   1961 Stockholm Closed Class 1:1

Chapter 2:   Letting the Seed Take Root
             #425   1961 Stockholm Closed Class 2:1

Chapter 3:   Attaining the Christ-Mind
             #424   1961 Stockholm Closed Class 1:2

Chapter 4:   The Temple
             #500   1962 Holland Closed Class 2:1

Chapter 5:   The Function of the Christ in Us
             #499   1962 Holland Class 1:1

Chapter 6:   What Have You in the House?
               #426   1961 Holland Special Class 1:1

Chapter 7:   Living Out From Conscious Oneness
               #500   1962 Holland Closed Class 2:2

Chapter 8:   Special Lesson on Healing Work
               #405   1961 Mission Inn Closed Class 5:2

Chapter 9:   The Spiritual Kingdom Made Tangible
               #499   1962 Holland Class 1:2

Chapter 10:   God Dominion: Not Man's Domination
               #444   1962 Hawaiian Village Open Class 1:1

Chapter 11:   Unconditioning the Mind
               #427   1961 New York Special Class 1:2

Chapter 12:   Spiritual Preparation for Peace
               #536   1963-64 Christmas-New Year's Message 1:1